Tricouleur

ABOUT THE BOOK

Raymond Betts is an absorbing writer who has tackled the subject of French colonialism with great skill and clarity. No other comprehensive study of the French overseas empire is now available in English.

A tale of individual heroism and collective blundering, the story of French colonial expansion reveals much of the best and the worst of French civilization. Built on commercial and political interest backed by military muscle, the empire arose without popular consent either at home or abroad. The origins of the Indochinese conflicts, Cambodia and Vietnam, and of the Algerian conflict, the building of the railways, the forced labour policies, the rise of the Third World nationalism, Le Corbusier's plans for Algiers, André Gide's articles on Equatorial Africa—Professor Betts tells the whole story. He casts a hard, realistic eye on the mixed bag of its achievement in tropical medicine, in supplying 700,000 soldiers to the French Army in World War 1, in providing cheap raw materials and cheap labour.

ABOUT THE AUTHOR

Raymond Betts is Professor of History at the University of Kentucky. His *False Dawn* about European Imperialism and *Europe Overseas: Phases Of Imperialism* were praised for their narrative fluency and significance. He has written or edited three other books and contributed numerous articles on French history to newspapers and magazines.

Tricouleur
The French Overseas Empire

Raymond Betts

Gordon & Cremonesi

Designed by Heather Gordon
Set in 11 on 13 pt Bembo
by Input Typesetting Ltd., London
and printed in Great Britain
by The Anchor Press Ltd
and bound by Wm Brendon & Son Ltd
both of Tiptree, Essex

British Library Cataloguing in Publication Data
Betts, Raymond F
    Tricouleur.
    1. France—Colonies—History
    1. Title
    909'.09'171244   JV1811   77-30503

LCCN: 77-030503
ISBN: 0-86033-060-5

Gordon & Cremonesi Publishers
London and New York
New River House
34 Seymour Road
London N8 OBE

FOR JAMES KING

A Warm Admirer

Of His Channel Neighbors

Acknowledgements

As with most every other book, this one was moved along by the encouragement and criticisms of several people. I wish to thank Professor William B. Cohen of Indiana University and Professor Kim Munholland of the University of Minnesota for their careful reading of the manuscript and for their judicious comments. The librarians at the University of Kentucky, and notably Mr Alexander Gilchrist, have helped with a number of details, some arcane, some simply elusive. My son, Kenneth, acted as a pictorial research assistant and found most of the photographs used in the book. Ms Terry VanDyke provided excellent secretarial service by typing the manuscript quickly and accurately. And this she did with good humor and much patience.

My wife, Jackie, read the manuscript with an eye to style and with an interest in this subject which we have shared in Europe, Africa, and at home.

It would be remiss of me not to include a few words of thanks to those many Frenchmen and Africans who helped me understand the French colonial experience and who taught me the truth of what I had long believed: that goodwill is a rich endowment of all peoples and cultures.

Contents

Preface   13
1 Planting the Flag   17
2 Late Nineteenth Century French
       Theories of Imperialism   37
3 The Definition of Empire   54
4 Empire in Fact   74
5 Empire in Form   97
6 From the Other Side   116
7 The Retreat from Empire   133
Afterward   150
Booknotes   158
Index   169

"Without knowing why, we render honors to the flag as if it carried the image of some titular divinity, as if some misfortune would accompany its loss. . . .

Denis Diderot in *L'Encyclopédie*

"We follow the flag of France without even concerning ourselves with whose hands hold it."

Cardinal Charles Lavigerie,
Missions d'Alger, 1883

"A flag is portable, and in this case there is hope that the flag which was raised in Fashoda was not the flag of France, but the flag of an individual explorer."

Lord Roseberry in a speech on the Fashoda Incident, given at Epsom, week of October 15, 1898

Preface

Ten years ago, on a summer afternoon, I was sitting on the beach of the island of Gorée, which lies about a mile off the West African coast and forms part of the sovereign territory of the Republic of Senegal. The sun had declined, the tide was out, and the beach was deserted except for a few Senegalese children. The setting was one that could easily have figured in a Maupassant short story.

I had been conversing in an idle sort of way with a *vieux colon*, one of those ageless Frenchmen who remained on the scene during the transition from colonial rule to national independence. We had talked of France and of Africa, and now our speech drifted off to sea. After a brief silence, the Frenchman questioned, as much to assure himself as to ask me, "It wasn't such a bad affair after all, was it, our African empire?" I shrugged my shoulders and pursed my lips in the fashion that foreigners so readily adopt from the French. What could I say?

There was then no simple answer to the question asked by the *vieux colon*, and there is still none today. The violence of our own times, the failure of meaningful social revolutions in almost all of the former colonial territories, and the appearance of new, continental imperialism, both in Africa and in Asia, deny any categorical assertion that European imperialism was a unique phenomenon or even the worst of modern institutionalized forms of oppression. Even some Africans and Asians have considered that the French should be more praised than damned for what they did. Certainly, the long line of tearful African heads of state who filed to Colombey-les-Deux-Églises after the death of General Charles de Gaulle was a mute and profound expression of some bond that economic materialists would be hard pressed to explain.

By that dreary November in France, it was all over. The famous
general who had bridged ages and governments also bridged continents. Empire ended during his Presidency—and without the anguish
that a less skilled, resolute, and historically-conscious individual
might have provoked.

Today the French are involved in other matters. Youth is more
concerned with rock music, automobiles, blue jeans, and unemployment than with the call to service in far-away places. And, with
colonial empire gone, the government, a victim of the topsy-turvy
situation of modern economics, finds itself somewhat beholden to the
new oil empires. True, the Foreign Legion holds on, but it is as
outdated as a Parisian's beret—and much less serviceable.

Henri Brunschwig, one of France's best-known colonial experts
and professor at the École Pratique des Hautes Études in Paris, once
told me that the French today have little interest in the old empire.
Unlike their British counterparts, he lamented, French students are
not inspired to discover that particular past which was contrived
overseas. If the number of French doctoral dissertations on the subject
is a meaningful form of measurement, Professor Brunschwig is correct. But French scholars have not neglected the history of the empire,
and they have provided a fine list of monographs that complements
the work done in Great Britain and the United States on the subject.
No doubt Professor Brunschwig is right in the main: there is a general,
popular disinterest.

And yet the subject has its attraction, rather as if it were dressed in
motley. Although French imperialist ideologues of a few decades ago
tended to romanticize and praise far beyond any acceptable limits,
there is today no need to commit the comparable fault of belittling and
excoriating. As with all human endeavors not calculated to be mis-
chievous, this one produced some accidental good and frequently
avoided deliberate evil. It was filled with mistakes, yet contained
many successes. It had its heroes, who might be so classified even by
critics today. And its villains were neither so numerous nor so clever as
those who thrust and boast and occupy the daily news in our less-
than-temperate age.

To say this is to argue against hastily-rendered moral judgment.
And it is also to remind us that colonial empire was of another age. It
belonged to an era of discordant transition characterized by rapid
industrial development and seemingly rapid political contraction, a
time when Europe had clearly become the "Old Continent." The rise
of new nations, the sudden psychological realization of the fixed
dimensions of our globe, and the perceived threats of an imminent
"mass age" defined by population and gross national produce—such

factors were joined in the minds of many so that imperialism was briefly accepted as a fact of contemporary life.

It is good that colonial empire is now over. Foreign rule is something we moderns find particularly distasteful, and usually with good reason. Moreover, colonial empire could not withstand the buffeting forces that have disturbed the world since 1945. Such empire was always a fragile affair and had even in its heyday an impermanent quality about it. But was it incidental to global history, as Malcolm Muggeridge has claimed, an activity that will hardly merit a footnote or two in a history text written a century or two hence? I strongly doubt such an outcome. Imperialism was a world-shaping and shaking force. Nothing has been quite the same since it crossed the many seas and oceans to occupy the several continents. That is reason enough for the average citizen in our global age to reflect upon it.

The text that follows is meant to be a general one, an introductory essay that briefly spans the history of modern French empire and yet concentrates on some of its more important problems. Obviously, in a work of such limited dimensions, the reader will view nothing that approaches the definitive or the heavily documented. Some of the traditional academic form—footnotes, most obviously—has been purposely omitted, in the hope of allowing for a more leisurely reading by a wider audience. This is a book designed to be read in a sitting or two, in an evening or two. It is a book that I hope will lead the reader to further reflection and scholarly investigation.

As with any author who proposes to evaluate such a vast topic, I find my intellectual indebtedness very heavy. In a series of "booknotes," individual bibliographical essays on the research undertaken for each chapter, I have acknowledged those works which have informed my thought and shaped my arguments.

The narrative that follows will surely show the extent of distorted caricature that lies in the old story of the two Englishmen, two Germans, and two Frenchmen who were stranded on a desert island. The Englishmen, we are informed, immediately established a bank; the Germans constructed a barracks. As for the Frenchmen, they argued. In point of fact, the Frenchmen who went overseas engaged in those other activities as well. And, accordingly, they have left behind—in addition to such cultural remnants as their language, the daily handshake, and a collection of post offices—a history worth attending.

Chapter One

Planting the Flag

Marquess Curzon of Kedleston, an imperial personage whose tone matched his bearing, offered this comment about one aspect of the French colonial effort: "In the spring of 1885 I was in Tunis. At no time in recent history a very interesting place, it had, since the French usurpation of 1881, lost what little characteristic individuality it then possessed."

Curzon's obvious implication was given even more direct expression by others of his countrymen who were writing in the late nineteenth century. In their own national press and also in the American, for which they then provided much of the foreign coverage, British commentators offered an extended list of terms describing French imperialism as inept or ignoble. The "vainest of dreams" were the words in which one commentator dismissed newly-expressed French imperial aspirations in 1885. "A vile intrigue" was Winston Churchill's succinct appraisal of France's march toward Fashoda in 1898. "France has no crowding populations . . . but on the boulevards of Paris alone enough writers could be found to fit out a thousand colonies" was still another author's cynical assessment of the French manly spirit of adventure, as defined in 1889. "A study of history . . . is more than enough to confirm an impartial observer in the generally accepted idea that the French cannot colonize" was a crisp summary statement appearing in an article published in 1884 by the well-known journal *Nineteenth Century*.

Such a review of British press commentary presents one segment of public opinion, yet one shared by many Frenchmen themselves. The apparent hesitancy with which the French engaged in colonial expansion in the 1880s was matched by argumentation over the matter among politicians at home. Nevertheless, the empire of the republic continued to grow, more by fits and starts than by leaps and bounds, it is true, but to impressive dimensions nonetheless. Shortly after the turn of the century the President of the Third Republic proudly claimed that continental France comprised but one twenty-third of the territory over which the tricolor was unfurled.

Even a public hitherto described as notoriously indifferent to colonial matters then responded to the magic of "empire." Colonial societies and congresses proliferated and colonial periodicals abounded, but the immense reality of it all was suggested by displays at the various international exhibitions, beginning with the one com-memorating the centenary of the French Revolution, but reaching imposing dimensions with the Colonial Exhibition of 1906 at Marseil-les, where samples of the many cultures found within overseas France were mounted in structures of exotic architecture. At Marseilles the visitors could see that the sun need not set on this empire anymore than on the one governed by the nation of shopkeepers situated on the other side of the Channel.

It appeared to happen quickly, this growth of empire and the belated enthusiasm that caught up with it. Furthermore, it seemed at first glance inconsistent with the general state of contemporary French society.

Viewed culturally, late nineteenth century France was not a hex-agon, but a *petit pré carré*. With a population that was static, an economy that was essentially agricultural, and a social situation that was primarily rural, the nation seemed at home with itself and gave no significant signs of an urgent need to seek fortune abroad. Moreover, domestic matters received precedence over foreign affairs. The recent defeat of the Second Empire by Bismarck's Prussia and allied German states dislodged France from a traditional position as keystone of the European state system and served as final proof of the follies of Napoleon III's foreign policy. In colonial affairs, the ill-starred empire of Maximilian in Mexico preceded the Franco-Prussian War by a few years and left military adventure in particular disfavor among the French public. What predominated in the 1870s were domestic and continental matters. The first concerned the establishment of a new republican government that would "divide us least." And the second concerned a territorial matter that was far more significant than any colonial one: the loss of Alsace and Lorraine to Germany. Some years later, during a debate in which overseas territory was proposed as possible compensation for the loss of these provinces, the poet Paul Déroulède stated contemptuously, "I have lost two daughters and you offer me twenty domestics."

In these formative years, if empire meant anything to Jacques

Prudhomme and his millions of continentally-fixed fellow patriots, it was as the place to which firebrands and the military might be directed, or from which such exotic items as coconuts, bananas, and carved jade elephants issued.

Not contained by these general conditions, the wave of "new imperialism" swept out from France, as it did from nearly every other European country in the last two decades of the nineteenth century. It was, as the great figure of French imperialism, Jules Ferry, described it, "an immense steeplechase toward the unknown." The excitement and pace suggested in Ferry's comment are those qualities which have led historians to retain the more familiar metaphor applied to this phenomenon: "scramble."

Certainly the rapidity of territorial annexation is qualitative difference enough to set late nineteenth century expansion off from the overseas activities that had occurred before it. French critics, writing at the time of the "new imperialism," had referred to territorial acquisition up to that time as a process of accumulating *petits paquets*. Indeed, to the casual observer, it seemed as if the French purchased in a random and careless manner. However, the geographical areas available were in reality confined. The general tropical situation of the new possessions set them apart from much of the territory of earlier empire. Moreover, their rather impressive populations and their generally well-articulated political structures contrasted with much of the *ancien régime's* colonial situation and forced an argument for historical discontinuity. Although some authors originally looked backward to the eighteenth century experience in order to move forward to the late nineteenth century one, most writers were in agreement that the new empire was not the old "New France." What had been lost in Canada and Louisiana could not be found elsewhere.

Nevertheless, it is important to note that French overseas activities had not ceased with the defeat of Montcalm on the Plains of Abraham outside Quebec in the year 1759. What occurred soon after this event was a shift in the locus of French interest from the New World to older worlds, those of Africa and Asia. As that astute statesman Talleyrand remarked in 1797, "If someday America becomes sufficiently powerful to regard as its own all the lands cast about on the New Continent, then think what advantages France will have if it has turned its eyes toward the Old World."

Talleyrand knew of what he spoke. It is true that France retained a few footholds in the New World—Martinique and Guadeloupe in the Caribbean, French Guiana, and the fishing islands of St Pierre and Miquelon in the North Atlantic; but the rest of her properties there were either negotiated or taken away, with the United States rising as arbiter of the Americas. Maximilian's puppet state in Mexico was the brief and tragic exception that proved the new rule of American guardianship.

Long before this diplomatic fiasco upset the foreign policy of Napoleon III, that goateed gentleman's balding predecessor had already packed his ambitions for shipment to Egypt. Napoleon I clearly heeded Talleyrand's advice.

The Egyptian campaign of 1798–9 had a particular drama of its own, what with the future emperor consulting the ever-silent Sphinx, and then fighting the Battle of the Pyramids, which enabled him to secure Cairo on July 22, 1798. However, Napoleon was only a summer tourist. He stayed more than a year in the land of the pharaohs and then turned his forces and their military fate over to another French general. By late March 1801 the French had unsuccessfully encountered their age-old and ubiquitous enemies, the British, who were then supporting, as they often were to do in the nineteenth century, the Ottoman Turks. The triumph of the British and their allies ended the French occupation.

However short-lived the French military presence in that land, it can be considered a pivotal point in French colonial history. Africa, the Levant, and the lands of Asia that lie far beyond were all brought into French political focus. "Mistress of Egypt," prophesied General Bonaparte, "France will in time be mistress of India."

This was never to be. However, Napoleon's overseas affairs remained of great importance. The occupation of Egypt in 1798 and the sale of Louisiana in 1803 mark the major geopolitical shift in French colonial history: the beginning of military dominion in Africa and Asia, the end of settlement colonies in America.

Well before the "scramble," therefore, the lines of French expansion were being sketched. It was Talleyrand who offered the preparatory remarks to modern French imperialism, just as it was Napoleon who provided the first significant action. Indeed, the military imperialism of Napoleon, defined in terms of prestige, glory, political power, and enmity toward Great Britain, soared, like the eagle by which it was symbolically represented, across the century and over lands that were oceans removed from continental France.

Yet such dramatic generalization should not be allowed to obscure the fact that a well-defined and sustained colonial policy was not to be found until the very end of the century.

It has been argued with considerable persuasiveness that most of French imperialism was belated governmental response to activities undertaken far away from Paris by individuals who frequently altered, defied, or simply ignored official policy. That irregular band of self-seekers and noble spirits, who were soldiers, merchants, explorers and missionaries, marched on to encounter problems that the home government then felt politically compelled to resolve.

This interpretation is given further credibility by the social nature of the nineteenth century universe. The French world, like that of the rest of Europe, was still locally and regionally defined. Time-distance was then measured in the beat of horsehoofs or the pressure of steam escaping from the pistons of lumbering railroad engines. Until late in the century, communications and transportation were so inadequate and slow that effective metropolitan control of any colonial situation was tenuous at best. Therefore, the man-on-the-spot had an independence that would have been peremptorily denied him at home. Moreover, until the end of the century France had no effective colonial administration, no sound method of recruiting personnel, and no well-established agency of governmental control over the colonies. To speak of any "system" is to talk of the hypothetical, not the historical. The reality of imperialism was in the singular person of the Frenchman who happened to be there.

To argue this is not to deny that initiative in colonial expansion did come from the home government and that nationally-determined policy was often carried out as closely to the letter as abilities, manpower and equipment would allow—not to mention the nature of local resistance encountered. But so frequently did the historical dialectic seem to move from overseas provocation to national solution that the local scene and its actors might best be regarded first.

France's expansion began early in the century and in a rather traditional way. Less than fifteen years after Napoleon was forcibly colonized by way of exile on the British possession of St Helena, the French were again involved in foreign adventure. In 1830, a French expeditionary force was sent to Algiers to avenge a diplomatic slight committed some time before—actually a slap with a fly swatter administered by the Dey of Algiers to the cheek of the French consul. The incident began as a classic example of sword-rattling, or of what would soon be called "gunboat diplomacy." However, the initial occupation, planned as a temporary affair of a few weeks, was extended into permanent domination, with the French military administering Algeria for four decades before civilian control was established.

Thus, the second colonial empire began, not in a "fit of absence of mind," of course, but without any clear assessment of possible consequences. The same imperialist situation was soon repeated half a world away. In the Far East, the French navy, suffering from a condition of anglophobia that had been intensified by the Battle of

Trafalgar, trafficked about in search of ports and esteem. Equally noticeable were the Catholic missionaries, who viewed the vast region as an ecclesiastical responsibility. However unnatural a combination, priests and sailors joined in a political logic of their own. What the Catholic missionaries desired was local acceptance of their activity; what the captains of the fleet desired was the assertion of their power. Frequently, missionary causes produced naval effects. The acquisition of Tahiti in 1843 was an outstanding example of this development, and so was the initial annexation of three provinces of Cochinchina, the southernmost portion of Indochina, in 1859. In brief, the religious difficulties the Catholic missionaries encountered, either harassment of their members or persecution of their local converts, provoked sufficient concern or excuse in France to require the government to take naval action.

Finally, in this process of piecemeal acquisition, the French again appeared on the west coast of Africa, from which region they had been ejected as a result of the Revolutionary and Napoleonic Wars. Gericault's painting "The Raft of the Medusa" memorializes this historical fact. In 1816 the frigate *Medusa* was carrying French personnel to St Louis in Senegal when it foundered. Initial French colonial efforts did not do much better. Not until the middle of the nineteenth century, when the military occupation of the hinterland seriously began, did the small commercial community on the coast sense security and anticipate profits. Farther south, but in a pattern of no great variance, the French navy was constructing a few forts and providing its units with a port of call at Gabon.

The preceding sketch has been drawn in much greater detail by a considerable number of historians, but even in its rough form it allows for one principal assertion. The reality of the then-existent French colonial world was rudely defined by the military. No other colonial empire belonging to a European nation was to have such a pronounced military character. Therefore, the military as agents of imperialism merit particular attention.

It would be easy to state that, in a century of generally peaceful bourgeois development, military prowess had less opportunity for display at home than hencetofore and was, accordingly, a prime talent for export. Such an argument was made by the Austrian economist Joseph Schumpeter in his famous *Imperialism and Social Classes*, first published in 1919. Therein he described imperialism as being the direct result of "military atavism," an age-old European military spirit that directed a modern state to "unlimited forcible expansion." The thesis is questionable at best, but not without some factual support. Certainly after 1870, when opportunity for advancement in France was minimal, officers found the most convenient path to promotion and the best road to glory somewhere in the bush or the jungle.

Furthermore, the very range of action afforded the colonial officer was an appeal. Conqueror, administrator, constructor—all these activities were there for the "colonial chief" who, by a stroke of his baton, "managed to have tilled a corner of the vast field available to human activity"—in the rhetoric of Hubert Lyautey, later Resident-General of Morocco and Marshal of France.

Some of these generalizations were translated into hard historical facts. Algeria began more as a military domain than as a settlement colony. Marshal Thomas Bugeaud, its major military commander and governor, stated his position emphatically in 1842: "The army is no less necessary for realizing the advantages of the conquest than for making it possible. It is and will remain for a long time to come the sole significant agent for the important operations that will open commercial lines, even the interior of Africa, to French commerce." Bugeaud's critics would complain that he spent more time on military campaign than in governance, but he retaliated that France's future in Algeria would remain precarious until military conquest were completed. And so he moved aggressively over the land, even once intruding into Morocco to defeat and disperse the Sultan's troops, whom he claimed were assisting the Algerians. It was this Battle of Isly in 1844 that gave Bugeaud his title, Duke of Isly.

Algeria was no peculiar instance. Military conquest and deployment pushed colonial frontiers outward in other regions. Senegal has been an often-cited instance. There, one of the most successful and respected colonial officers, Louis Faidherbe, began an empire where previously there had been only a precariously-situated colony. Until his military push, the French were restricted to a few coastal stations and to local commerce, primarily gum rubber, along the Senegal River. It was Faidherbe who mapped out a military strategy in the 1850s that would mark a half-century of colonial expansion in the area. This was done to the disadvantage of a regional Moslem empire, dominated by the Tokolors, and ruled by an able military and religious leader, El-Hadj Omar. Some critics have seen the resulting clash between French and Tokolors as the entanglement of two competing imperialisms. The assessment is, of course, an appraisal of African history in European terms, but it remains as good a brief analysis as will be found. Faidherbe did not destroy Omar's power; he greatly reduced it and forced a military retreat.

For all this, the government of the Second Empire and then that of the Third Republic did not view these military operations with much enthusiasm or interest. West Africa was not a center of national

interest, and extended involvement there, it was thought, could result
in national dissipation, not enlargement. Not until late in the century
did French imperialism again spread further into the hinterland, and
then it did so in strictly military terms.

Under the command of a series of able, ambitious military commanders who preferred action to negotiation and who found Parisian
temporizing a form of tampering, Senegal was advanced in size, and a
new set of colonies was carved inland. In the words of Colonel
Borgnis-Desbordes, military commander of the newly-created command of Upper Senegal, in 1880, what was needed was the "go-ahead
des Américains," an energetic push onward. This was later provided
by one of the most striking of the military imperialists, Colonel Louis
Archinard, when he undertook the destruction of the two major
Islamic kingdoms in the area: the decaying Tokolor Empire, by then
under the rule of Omar's son Ahmadou; and the more powerful and
significant empire of Samory, located on the right bank of the Niger
and extending to the limits of the Tokolor Empire.

Full of plausible explanations and personal ambitions, between
1888 and 1890 Archinard improvised a local political situation meant
to suggest to the home government the need for military action
against the two empires. The details of Archinard's manipulations are
an intriguing little history in themselves—the story of his efforts to
convince the government in Paris that military advancement was both
feasible and necessary. Previous military operations undertaken by
Archinard against the Tokolors had been unapproved and in direct
violation of treaty arrangements. But his assault on the capital, Segou,
was given tacit approval, if not enthusiastic endorsement. After
quickly completing this task, in 1890, he plunged farther into the
Sudan and the Tokolor Empire, extending his territorial acquisitions,
just as he did his personal authority, beyond anything the government
had contemplated. Nor did he then stop. In flagrant violation of
government policy, he launched an attack on the more formidable
empire of Samory, thus initiating a new chapter in local military
imperialism that would continue until the final defeat of Samory's
forces in 1898.

After West Africa, such military initiative in imperial affairs next
found expression in Morocco. Morocco, in the first decade of the
twentieth century, acquired new political proportions, both as a diplomatic issue and as a border problem. The setting of contending
European spheres of influence, particularly French and German, the
country had also—in French opinion—caused frontier difficulties, by
tribal incursions into its neighbor to the east, Algeria. As already
noted, Bugeaud sent a force into Morocco in 1844. Moreover, geo-

graphical contiguity between the two lands had led the French Foreign Minister, Théophile Delcassé, to state in 1901 that France had "a special interest" in Morocco.

Hubert Lyautey entered this general situation and added to it a new military dimension. Assigned to the military command of South Oran, a border region where skirmishes between Moroccan tribesmen and French soldiers were occurring in the very first years of the new century, Lyautey responded to this friction in a military way and on no authority but his own. In 1904 he sent into Morocco a military expedition, which despite the French government's official demand that the force immediately retire, occupied the oasis of Ras-el-Ain. After weeks of negotiation, Lyautey responded as requested. However, by then Franco-Moroccan relations had further deteriorated, with the Sultan doubting French pledges that Moroccan sovereignty would be maintained.

Brief, militarily effective, the Ras-el-Ain episode was something of a classic piece, the imperial "border incident." Anything but a uniquely French phenomenon, the border incident was a frequent provocation for the extension of colonial rule, as witness the British in the Punjab or, much later, the Italian Fascists in Ethiopia. Marauding tribes versus defending colonial troops—such was the usual political equation presented to the home government whose support was elicited.

No doubt this action on the frontier projected a certain romantic quality before nineteenth century European eyes, often a *beau geste* of dedication and of "service beyond the call of duty"—or in opposition to prescribed definitions of it. One can find, in the annals of French colonial history, no better examples of this sort of individualized behavior than those afforded by François Garnier and Henri Rivière. As if in tandem, these two men performed similar military actions in the same setting, with the same disregard for orders, with the same disastrous personal results and in the same geographical situation— almost exactly a decade apart.

Garnier, an explorer, author, and naval officer, had high hope for the development of trade with South China through the Red River and the Gulf of Tonkin, along the Vietnamese "borders" with the Celestial Empire. He was sent on an expedition by the governor of Cochinchina to open Tonkin to French trade and to establish French influence with the court of the Emperor of Annam. However, in 1873, faced with opposition, Garnier used his military force to assault the citadel of Hanoi, which guarded the Red River route. This successful operation was negated by his own death shortly thereafter. As for the furtherance of French imperialism, all that came of this effort was a vague treaty of protectorate, so formed because the government in Paris disavowed any intentions of conquering Annam and, furthermore, considered Garnier's death an irreparable military loss.

Ten years later, in 1883, Henri Rivière re-enacted the scenario. Rivière, too, was a naval officer and an esteemed writer. In truth, his writing was better known and more highly regarded than his military career, which had so far proved undistinguished; and, at the age of fifty-four, he seemed unlikely to improve much on this record.

Now the general chaos in Tonkin brought him briefly to the forefront of French colonial affairs. Since Garnier's death, nothing had improved, as far as the French could see, and their influence even seemed impaired. Therefore, Rivière was charged by the Governor of Cochinchina, and with the approval of the home government, to have another go at establishing French influence. At the time, the Black Flags, so named because of the standards they carried, had become particularly bothersome as they roamed the region in search of loot— and out of dislike of the French presence. A well-armed mercenary band, they presented a serious problem to the Emperor of Annam, who ruled Tonkin. Curiously, the Black Flags were also seen by this high personage as an element that might be placed in opposition to the French. The Emperor, therefore, complained about them and yet conspired to use them. Moreover, the Chinese government also availed itself of the activities of the Black Flags, by seizing on them as an excuse to send regular troops into Tonkin.

Complicated in its Asian setting, and befuddling in France, where other imperial problems demanded attention, the Tonkinese situation rested on the shoulders and wit of Rivière for immediate solution. The commander was firmly informed that he should not use force, only diplomatic persuasion, to re-establish French influence. Again, events did not turn out as expected, though certainly repetitious in their consequences. Fearing attack, Rivière assaulted the citadel of Hanoi on May 26, 1882, and took it. The Chinese were indignant, the French officials in Cochinchina were disturbed, but the Parisian press approved. Meanwhile, Rivière moved forward militarily in the delta region, once more in defiance of instructions. His melodramatic end occurred when he attacked some 15,000 Black Flags with 750 soldiers of his own on May 19, 1883. The tragic symmetry which held together the careers of Garnier and Rivière was maintained until the end. Rivière fell in death near where Garnier had fallen before him.

Out of this confusion and its immediate disaster, the French occupation of Annam and Tonkin was seriously undertaken. A substantial expeditionary force, for which the French parliament voted funds, redressed the military situation to French satisfaction, and a treaty of protectorate was signed with Annam on August 25, 1883.

Here, then, was another example of military imperialism, unintended at first, certainly by Rivière. Border or frontier incidents and imbroglios were frequent in modern French expansion. They are also easily defined historically, which is not the case with any historical evaluation of the events transpiring in less belligerent settings, such as the bank, the board-room, or the factory.

Although the French economy revealed few of those signs that, according to later Marxist interpretations, made imperialism a categorical imperative, trade and empire had their connections. Even before large-scale expansion began, the *comptoirs* on the west coast of Africa, the enclaves of India—Pondicherry, for instance—were like points on a diagram, suggesting how new economic interests might be assembled. Moreover, some intrepid merchant-adventurers, such as the firm of Régis Frères of Marseilles, were staking out new commercial territories, in this instance on the Ivory Coast. At home, economic interest was also aroused. If the nation expressed little pleasure over the invasion of Algiers in 1830, Marseilles merchants watched the encounter with anticipation of expanding markets. The city of Lyons, gaining fame in the nineteenth century for its missionary efforts, also went abroad in search of new commerce and therefore supported French involvement in Indochina. As silk center of France, Lyons had a particular concern with Far Eastern trade. Moreover, when in the 1860s disease destroyed the vast majority of silk cocoons in France, Lyonnais merchants investigated the possibilities of Syria as a source of raw materials and thus further directed French interests toward the Levant.

Alongside trade grew capital investments abroad. Egypt, no longer a French parade-ground, attracted French financiers, who invested heavily in state bonds, the money of which was primarily used, in the middle of the century, to realize the building projects of the Khedive Ismael Pasha. And the Suez Canal was dug primarily with Parisian capital, resulting in further French financial commitment to the country.

Bond-selling across North Africa, from Egypt in the east to Morocco in the west, was an attractive European financial activity, not diminished even when debt-ridden governments threatened to default. In the second half of the century, however, European debt commissions were established to see that the heavy, and ever-increasing, interest on the loans was regularly paid. Default on bond issues was a principal reason why both France and Britain contemplated gaining control of the government in Egypt. It later was the chief

justification for the continuation of British domination of Egypt, after
the country had been invaded in 1882.

The French occupation of both Tunisia in 1881 and Morocco in
1912 was prefaced by financial activities. Both countries were ruled by
extravagant, luxury-minded individuals, who happily and unwit-
tingly indebted themselves to Europeans. In Tunisia, the first loan, a
British–French venture, was made in 1863, at a time when interest
rates in the European market were very low. Soon, in 1866, the beylic
government was bankrupt, presenting a cause of some concern to the
French investors and government. In 1867 the French Foreign Minister toyed with the idea of asserting French political control over
Tunisia, perhaps through a protectorate; but an Italian–British sugges-
tion to establish an International Debt Commission terminated this
idea. Similar developments occurred in Morocco, although there, at
the beginning of the twentieth century, the French government also
encouraged, even requested, business involvement, as a means of
assuring French penetration of the region. The great French steel
company headed by Schneider founded a Moroccan subsidiary, which
enhanced French "interests" in the country and showed itself a willing
agent of the national government.

Such financial aggressiveness in the soon-to-be-colonial world
amounted to exceptional performance by French capitalists.
Nineteenth century French capital generally sought less exotic settings. Heavy investment in North and South America occurred, and
French capital followed the flag northward to Russia at the time of the
Franco-Russian Alliance of 1893–4. Moreover, investments in Eastern
Europe were more significant than in the overseas empire. Even when
the rubber industry was growing, in the early twentieth century,
French capital preferred British Malaya to French Indochina. Many
imperialists would lament what they considered to be excessive caution on the part of French capitalists where French overseas territories
were concerned. Furthermore, in local colonial commerce the lack of
French initiative was frequently berated. Such was the case in Senegal,
where the decision to expand territorially to protect French trade in
face of a rapidly developing British commerce in the Niger region
came from the military, who found French coastal merchants of a
sluggish disposition in business matters.

Related to the economics of empire was technological planning.
Here, at least, the French were bolder in conception. Whether they
read and accepted the schemes of Jules Verne or not, many French
engineers imagined vast communications networks binding and
bridging continents. There is no doubt that the railroad was the
geometric principle of imperial thought, as technicians mapped out

Trans-Saharan and then Trans-African systems. Less imposing but much more real was the construction, in 1882–5, of the first railroad in West Africa, which was about 150 miles long and ran between St Louis and Dakar in Senegal. Elsewhere the railroad was a factor in French imperial involvement. The French-owned Bône–Guelma railroad line in Tunisia was one of the French interests that preceded and influenced the occupation of 1881, just as the many small French-owned railroads in Syria were elements extending French influence in the Near East at the beginning of the twentieth century. The French politician and avid imperialist Gabriel Hanotaux once remarked that the railway station was more valuable than the fort in the process of colonization.

The growing concern with technology gave to physical space a different dimension. Both the United States and the British Empire represented new geographical systems that the French respected, often wanted to imitate. Perhaps it is no coincidence that Jules Verne's marvelous fictional essay on the historical process of technological growth, *The Mysterious Island*, ended with the island-stranded heroes establishing a model community in the state of Iowa in the American Midwest. New conceptions of what the French could do in the expanding colonial world helped condition, if they did not directly cause, modern imperialism. In 1912 the French politician Albert Messimy wrote a brief article in the *Revue de Paris* which nicely supports this point. Reviewing the fact that the Eiffel Tower had been in direct radio contact with Casablanca since 1907, he announced that "Africa must become the center of our worldwide telegraphic communication system." Imperial thinking, in this new age of technology, was global thinking.

And yet global thinking most often followed well-established nineteenth century nationalist patterns. If there is a classic interpretation of France's modern overseas expansion, it is one cast in nationalist terms. In simple statement it asserts that military defeat in Europe was transmuted into political incentive abroad. France, in an effort to demonstrate to the world that the nation was only humiliated, not subdued, by the German victory of 1870–1, sought glory and prestige abroad. French nationalists became imperialists.

There is no doubt that the political factor, of which nationalism is a powerful expression, worked into all aspects of modern French imperial activities. International politics, invisibly regulated by the "balance of power," held the attention of patriotic Frenchmen, who viewed in distress the ascendancy of Germany in Europe, the still-serene paramountcy of Great Britain in the world, and the sudden and noisy appearance of the United States on the shores of the Pacific. Moreover, by 1898 the French were provided with what appeared to be an object lesson in history, as they looked toward the Caribbean to observe the final collapse of the once-powerful Spanish Empire.

No ardent French politician wished history to stop at the Rhine as it had at the Pyrennes. France's mission, in the nationalist rhetoric of the day, was necessarily global. Necessarily, because in the thought of these men the history of the nation and the influence of the imagined Latin tradition which had always mantled it now styled the foreign policy of the new republic as they had that of the monarchies and empires preceding it.

Through the tricolored lens that magnified the past, everything was elegantly, perhaps symmetrically arranged. The idea of *grandeur*, both a military and a cultural concept, is an old component of French foreign policy—as is the Whig tradition in British history and the frontier tradition in American. But these collective moods or attitudes are "real"—historically effective—only in so far as they are translated into political policy and action.

The heavy thread that strings together French international and colonial policy at the end of the nineteenth century is the continuing rivalry with Great Britain. "France and England, having diametrically opposite interests, are and will be, by the very nature of things, rivals" wrote Jean Darcy in *France et Angleterre: Cent ans de rivalité*, published in 1904. Victor Bérard, another colonial enthusiast, was both more specific and bitter. "It is a tradition;" he stated in his *Angleterre et l'impérialisme*, appearing in 1900, "France gets colonies in order that John Bull may take them." At the same time as abuse was being heaped on Great Britain for its worthiness of the name "Perfidious Albion," praise was being bestowed on the British for their imperial spirit, sound colonial administration, and successful commercial policy abroad. Lastly, alongside the rivalry ran a near century-long spirit of entente, of cooperation frequently arrived at in the Near and Far East. The Crimean War of 1856 was one obvious manifestation of such cooperation, as was joint military action against China in 1852, to get that country to open further to European trade. Palmerston expressed the English attitude toward the concept of entente when he said, "England and France have many interests, commercial and political, all over the world which are perpetually coming into contact, and a good understanding between Paris and London is necessary."

It is doubtful that there ever was an era of "good understanding" between Great Britain and France, even in those years of the Entente Cordiale, when the bonvivance of King Edward VII at least gave the outward appearance of British enjoyment of things French. In the nineteenth century, points of friction between the two countries could be found around the globe, going from rival naval and missionary interests in the Pacific, to conflicting commercial policies in the Niger and Congo river areas, and on to fishing rights off the coast of Newfoundland. The French navy engaged in its own spirited imperialism along the coast of Southeast Asia and West Africa, as a means of exorcising the anglophobia that had bedevilled it particularly since Trafalgar. Later, the military expeditions of an exploratory sort that were thrust into Central Africa were in part an effort to frustrate the British there and certainly drew inspiration from the anti-British sentiment of some of their participants. Jean-Baptiste Marchand, leader of the famous expedition that crossed Africa from Gabon to the Sudan, arriving in Fashoda in 1898, was known to be more virulently opposed to the British than to France's newer and more threatening enemies, the Germans.

Much of French African policy at the end of the nineteenth century was conditioned, even provoked, by concern—fear and anger—over the policy pursued by Great Britain. The center of the rivalry was a country in which cooperation initially seemed possible. This was Egypt.

Despite Napoleon's hasty departure in 1799, French influence had persisted in Egypt. That first modernizer of Egypt, Mehemet Ali, who established his own dynasty of pashas at the beginning of the nineteenth century, enlisted French technical aid to build up his land. French education was introduced, French finances flowed in, and French enterprise helped construct modern Cairo, to say nothing of the later efforts made by Ferdinand De Lesseps.

This historical priority did not, however, replace the one maintained by the British in the form of a "lifeline of empire." The route to India by way of the Mediterranean was an important one, to which the canal added a new dimension. This dirt monument to French ingenuity, paid for by French money, maintained by a French company, and opened with great solemnity by a French empress, really was a British convenience. That British financiers had not supported the construction, even though they had been asked to, was an error recognized in hindsight. Benjamin Disraeli corrected the matter when in 1875 he purchased the financially distraught Khedive's shares.

Thereafter, the canal and the continuing profligate ways of the Khedive Ismael were major factors in Anglo-French cooperation in the land: the investment in the former, the loans to the latter were obvious bonds of gold. To complicate matters from the European standpoint, a proto-nationalist movement led by a military officer, one Colonel Arabi, threatened what little stability the Egyptian government had. Arabi opposed the foreign presence and the new pasha that the French and British had imposed; furthermore, he and his

fellow officers were irritated by the military cutbacks that the dwindl-
ing national treasury now required. This combination of factors suggested the need for some forceful European action.

A proposed joint naval display to be made by both French and
British units was not mounted as originally planned, because at the last
moment the French hesitated to take such action. Therefore, the
British navy alone made its presence known, and by more than an
appearance off the coast. On July 11, 1882, the British commander
fired his guns on Alexandria, in protest against warlike activities he
detected there. Then, four days later, British troops landed, seized the
canal, and undertook a temporary occupation that lasted some forty
years.

The hesitant French role in all of this grand-scaled gunboat diplomacy was the result of government instability at home. The ministry
of Léon Gambetta, who strongly favored the Egyptian venture, fell at
a crucial moment. Gambetta's successor as Premier, Charles de
Freycinet, was no less interested in involving France, but a recalcitrant
parliament refused the funds he requested for this participation. France
politically defaulted and, consequently, lost its political position in
Egypt. But the humiliation and the irritation that the British go-it-
alone policy brought to the politicians of the Third Republic cannot be
underestimated. The increase of British influence in Northeast Africa,
its extension into the Sudan, and the failure of the British to evacuate
Egypt quickly, as they had protested they would, made the Egyptian
question a major French diplomatic concern, its solution something of
a persistent issue.

French efforts continued to be frustrated till the end of the century,
when, changing its strategy, the government decided on a rather bold
and potentially dramatic action: the sending of an expedition across
the African continent to assure a French presence in the Upper Nile
and thereby to frighten the British, with the anticipated result of
dissuading them from further occupation of Egypt. The first two
missions charged with this responsibility failed, but the third, the
famous Marchand mission, trudged onward from Gabon to Fashoda,
a feat that required two years to complete.

However gallant, Marchand's effort was to no avail, and French
strategy consequently failed. The arrival of the ponderous military
cavalcade led by Lord Kitchener, who had just defeated a major
religious–military force in the Sudan, the Mahdists, led to government confrontation. For a brief moment war seemed in sight. But the
French, unsupported by other nations—in contrast with what they
had hoped—were left with little alternative but to endure another
humiliation. The two commanders raised their glasses in an appropri-

ate toast, Marchand lowered the tricolor, Kitchener raised the union flag, and thus the "Fashoda Incident" ended with this little ceremony performed on a meander in the River Nile.

The last region of encounter between these two colonial rivals was Morocco. Unable to dislodge the British from Egypt, either by diplomatic pressure or by military threats, the French government, through the skills of its Foreign Minister, Théophile Delcassé, sought a *quid pro quo* of sorts: British recognition of French interests in Morocco in return for French recognition of British interests in Egypt. This diplomatic maneuvering was of neither a random nor an erratic sort, however. France had long been involved in Moroccan affairs, and the thought of a well-rounded North African empire had some appeal. Moreover, Delcassé had been urged on by the "colonial party," an informal group of interested politicians, explorers and businessmen who had frequent banquets together, who sponsored the various colonial societies, and whose parliamentary membership frequently met in informal caucus on pending legislative business concerning the empire. The "colonial party," as recent historians have shown, was a significant element in French expansion: now molding the Moroccan question, it earlier had been financially and strategically behind the Marchand mission.

Convinced by the arguments he heard from members of the "colonial party," Delcassé moved to regulate this last North African issue. The outcome was the Entente Cordiale of 1903–4, one of the most well-known diplomatic understandings of the day. What the agreement did was clear away most of the chief matters at issue between France and Britain—Morocco and Egypt being the most important. The terms of the Entente regarding these two lands were straightforward: France agreed not to interfere with British activities in Egypt "by asking that a limit be fixed for the British occupation or in any other matter," and, in return, Great Britain recognized the fact that French colonial proximity to Morocco gave the French primary authority to maintain order there. British enthusiasm for the Entente was not matched in degree by the French. To some French politicians, the arrangement seemed one-sided. "We exchange rights for hopes," remarked a former Resident-General of Tunisia, René Millet. But in 1912 those hopes also became rights.

This brief review of British–French entanglements highlights an important aspect of the politics of modern French empire. If France and Great Britain were the two primary colonial powers, they shared no parity in early twentieth century global affairs. Great Britain and Germany were much stronger than was France, so that empire now became a buttress for France's "great-power" status. Accommodation with Great Britain made sense in face of the sword-rattling of Kaiser Wilhelm II and the concern that another war might break out. On the other side, Great Britain could no longer afford the myth of "splendid isolation." Of course, the British had never decided to tend strictly to their tidy little islands, but now their ability to manipulate world affairs was greatly circumscribed. Both France and Great Britain profited from the Entente Cordiale. In colonial matters, it effectively allayed, if it did not completely remove, the antagonism between the two countries. For, even as the Entente was being implemented, the French remained suspicious of British activities in Syria and Lebanon, two portions of the Ottoman Empire in which France had long diplomatic, cultural, and economic interests. In truth, subsequent difficulties France had with Syria as a mandated territory after the World War were frequently ascribed to British meddling. And so the matter of "spheres of influence," areas in which one nation hoped to have informal paramountcy, still disturbed official amity.

Yet the guns that roared on August 4, 1914, carried no particular colonial message. France had satisfied her few colonial problems with Germany, notably by an agreement of 1911, whereby a portion of Congo, the so-called *bec de canard*, was ceded to Germany in return for German recognition of France's claims to Morocco. Moreover, the most ardent of French imperialists were quite content with what they saw in 1914. "The day when the Moroccan question is resolved ... France will have accomplished its colonial work in Africa," Eugène Étienne, former Under-Secretary of State for Colonies, had remarked in 1903. And, while Joseph Chailley-Bert, an ardent imperialist propagandist, had said in 1908 that France should have taken Siam half a century earlier rather than engage in follies like the Crimean War, he, too, was satisfied with France's colonial outlook, even though a nominally free Siam still faced French Indochina.

When the war broke out, it aroused no major popular fears over the state of the empire. French militarists expected nothing from it, and the imperialists only wanted to hold on to it. The public agonized over the precarious condition of the northern departments of France itself. Yet there were some areas of concern which occupied official attention. Morocco was far from securely controlled, and the withdrawal of French troops left the country weakly defended. Then, when the Ottoman Empire entered the war in 1915, on the side of the Germans, French colonial officials in West Africa wondered whether Islam would prove to be an overriding force, ripping away the loyalty of the population under French domination. Finally, and most importantly, there was the question of what military attitude should be taken in Africa where German and French colonies were adjacent. The

French government opted for attack, and soon the weakly defended colonies of Togoland and Cameroon fell to the French.

The fact that the war was a European war was not lost on contemporaries and cannot be overstressed in retrospect. What mattered dearly to the French was taking place on the Western Front. Nevertheless, the turn of events in the Near East attracted some diplomatic attention as, once again, the "Sick Man of Europe" had a major seizure, this time properly diagnosed as fatal. The disintegration of the Ottoman Empire caused the French government to seek an accord with Great Britain about the distribution of the various pieces. In 1916 Sir Mark Sykes and Georges Picot, as representatives of their two governments, worked out the now famous Sykes–Picot agreement by which future spheres of influence were designated, with the French obtaining what later would be Syria and Lebanon. Thus, the last territorial issue of some concern between the two colonial powers was settled on paper.

Following the traditional procedures of all wars, the fate of Germany's colonies was in the hands of the victors. Within the framework of the League of Nations a mandates system was arranged, an institution that was a major step in what one Belgian historian has called "the internationalization of the colonial phenomenon." Instead of being annexed outright, an approach that would have consorted ill with Wilsonian idealism, control of these territories was "mandated" to other powers, notably France and Britain, and the "mandatory power" was required to give an annual accounting of its behavior and activities in the form of a report to the League of Nations. Arranged in categories defined according to European perceptions of their near-readiness for independence, the mandated territories had next to no say in the arrangements concerning their future. Thus, Syria, whose leaders were opposed to being mandated to France, fell under French control nonetheless—and subsequently caused the French a bundle of administrative problems. Lebanon, soon defined as a separate state, Togo and the Cameroon were all added to the French colonial empire.

It would not be considered historically distortive to view the peace negotiations as the last major act of European expansion. The French Empire, like the British, grew as a result of the war, with the League of Nations legitimizing a different form of indirect rule, but colonial rule nevertheless. By 1919, accordingly, Overseas France had reached its outer limits. These were impressive. With the addition of the new mandated territories, some 12,500,000 square kilometers of land were ruled by the Third Republic—an incredible mosaic of typography and cultures, portions of which were found in all the major oceans of the world and on all the major continents.

In the interwar period Frenchmen would speak of the colonial empire as if it were a fact of life, not a historical development. Pierre Lyautey, in his popular *L'Empire colonial français*, published in 1931, stated, "French expansion is an enduring and permanent phenomenon which has its rebirths and declines, its springtimes and its autumns, as well as its winters." This rhetorical flourish did not prohibit Lyautey from providing a good historical analysis, but it nonetheless represents a state of mind that at the time often made critical analysis of the causes of empire difficult.

To identify the French nation as a collectivity and French history as a continuum with late nineteenth century expansion was to risk distortion. If anything, the empire was created without national inspiration or dedication. Of minimal cost to the tight-pursed French taxpayer, of little disturbance to the politics of the new republic, and of little concern to the public at large, imperialism was the passion of a small number of dedicated nationalists, a no-more-impressive number of ambitious soldiers, and, as the century closed, a few ministers of state. Only sporadically was the public at large aroused to enthusiasm or anger. The constant outward concern of Frenchmen in the modern era has been the "Blue Line of the Vosges." But the shape of empire did not go unnoticed.

Chapter Two

Late Nineteenth Century French Theories of Imperialism

As the nineteenth century gave way to the twentieth, French polemicists rejoiced in the thought of a new era of popular support for empire. Joseph Chailley-Bert, then reigning as the most prolific of writers on the subject, asserted in 1899,

> Colonial policy is no longer the conception of a group of self-interested merchants, or of a clear-sighted governmental aristocracy. It has become a national thought ... and it will succeed because it is legitimate, necessary, wise, and sound—and because in guaranteeing the future greatness of France, it also contributes to stability and peace in the world.

However rhetorical may have been his insistence on the virtue of empire, he was essentially correct in saying that it had become a subject of national interest. Indeed, the ideology of French imperialism had now acquired a coherence, direction and public favor that were not evident even ten years earlier.

Nevertheless, there is little that was original in the explanations and rationalizations mustered to support French expansion. Most of it had been said either elsewhere, before, or more stirringly. The British orchestrated their imperial endeavors to the music of Sir Edward Elgar and the poetry of Rudyard Kipling, and the French had no national equivalent of either. The Germans could manfully insist upon their place in the sun and limber Krupps weapons to prove that they could easily obtain it, while the French, still chafing from defeat, hoped their colonies would be a source of military revitalization. The Americans exceeded their usual quota of superlatives when they read sermons on "manifest destiny" and westward-moving frontiers, but the French generated some pride in their Roman heritage and cast themselves in the role of modern Centurions guarding the frontiers of empire on sand-dunes in the Sahara.

Even when most stridently expressed, French imperialist ideology had an apologetic tone about it, the realization by its exponents that French suzerainty in the world was now strictly a matter of historical consideration, and the further realization that the greatness of French civilization had been generated in an age when literature and philosophy predominated, not in an age of steam and steel. Put otherwise, French imperialism was seen not as the expansion of a new nation, but as the possible regeneration of an old one.

Moreover, in the years in which it was being formulated, the ideology was haunted by the argument that the French had no *génie colonisateur*, no national ability to colonize. Proponents of new empire had the history of the old empire to live down or build up. They had to make something of it, and some did in a number of historical studies, most of which blamed the monarchical government, not any particular qualities of the French people, for the failure of that earlier enterprise. In addition, the same persons had to contend with the well-known stay-at-home, or *casanier*, spirit, proved by the small amount of emigration from France and by comments such as the following, from the American magazine *Outlook* of May 8, 1897: "The race suffers from nostalgia when it is far from France." Finally, the half-century of military colonization in Algeria and the more recent efforts at penal colonization in New Caledonia won the acclaim of few at home or abroad.

If French imperialists were thus compelled to account for history and to explain away tradition, they also rose above these issues to the realm of praise for those grand ideas and attitudes that were said to determine France's destiny and to confer upon the nation a particular "vocation." Much of what French imperialists such as Chailley-Bert said in 1899 General De Gaulle would be able to say—with some deletions, granted, but with no lessening of enthusiasm—some sixty years later. Such was the strength of certain myths about French civilization and national character.

To begin with, French expansion had long been considered a condition of the mind, if not of the body politic. "Our peculiar quality is our universalism" stated the twentieth century Thomistic philosopher Étienne Gilson, who thus tidily summed up an attitude that permeated the Enlightenment, the French Revolution, and later colonial policy. Priding themselves on their rational spirit and insisting that their language had a clarity and logic which allowed it to be the *lingua franca*, many French nationalists singled out France's cultural imperialism as its outstanding, praiseworthy quality. Wrote the novelist Maurice Barrès in 1906, "The preponderance of ideas, and the empire of the mind and of the heart, these are our goals. To others, primacy of finance or business, but to us, first and always, love of humanity."

The national emphasis on reason as the universal human trait and the national tendency toward administrative centralization, conceptualized in the Revolutionary notion of "the republic one and indivisible," biased French imperialism with a tradition of theoretical uniformity and a moral assertion that equality within the French scheme of things was a desirable objective. From the famous motto of the French Revolution, *fraternity* and *equality* would be extended overseas, but not by the agency of personal *liberty*. Rather, the direction and progress toward these two objectives would be determined by the French in their capacity of schoolmasters to the world, not as revolutionaries.

In terms of colonial ideology, this general attitude was translated by the words *mission civilisatrice*. The most arrogant justification for domination was just this proposed form of eventual acculturation: the "civilizing" of peoples whose way-of-life seemed, from a Parisian perspective, to be primitive, barbarian, or even non-existent. As Senator Charles Humbert, a member of the pro-colonial contingent in parliament, put it in 1912, "To develop the local populations, to make them evolve toward a civilization that they could not imagine themselves, this is what must be our constant objective, our highest goal."

The particular French colonial policy which such thought had already generated bears the name *politique d'assimilation*. It professed as intention the conversion and ultimate absorption of the peoples of the colonial world into the French nation. In its most outlandish form, the notion of a France grandly rounded off at 100,000,000 worldwide inhabitants, the totality radiating from Paris, was advertised as the forthcoming majestic creation of the French colonial effort. Thus, in theory, Wolofs, Annamites, Berbers, and Malagasy would all be made Frenchmen, invited to enjoy the privileges of that civilization and society. "Our ancestors, the Gauls, were flaxen-haired and blue-eyed" was the first lesson the history primer would teach one and all—or so critics of the theory cynically remarked.

Of course, the gap between grand principle and petty reality was enormously great. No French colonial official ever anticipated that social and political equality could exist between colonizer and colonized. Even as the colonial empire was being formed, assimilation was attacked as pretentious, nonsensical, and inapplicable to a situation in which the cultural differences and divergence of economic interests between the juxtaposed peoples, French and colonial, were so obvious.

But such rejection of assimilation as colonial policy did not alter the basic belief in France's generous collective spirit. The most influential study of the French Empire published between the two world wars, Albert Sarraut's *Mise en valeur des colonies françaises* (1923), contained among its prefatory remarks the following: "What characterized its [France's] colonial policy and gives it its particular definition, is its sense of humanity; it proceeds essentially from the great idea of human solidarity."

Below this metaphysical principle, charming and vain, were a number of elements that gave to French imperialist ideology more immediacy; they were much more narrowly defined historically, but not always much more realistically.

The first, because the most persistent and bothersome to contemporaries, was the apparently precarious national condition of France in an emerging age of global politics. Military defeat by Germany, demographic stagnation, bourgeois lassitude, and insufficient economic growth were all problems and levers used by the imperialists to arouse concern over empire. In the idiom of late nineteenth century national character analysis, France seemed to be suffering from a collective inferiority complex. "Neurasthenia" was a word much in vogue at the time, and it then suggested a sense of national fatigue, uneasiness, doubt—general nervous disorder.

No matter in which direction they looked, imperialists found cause for alarm abroad. Frightening comparisons were made between France and Britain as colonial builders and competitors. Awe was registered when the dimensions of continental France were compared with those of Russia or the United States. And, however reluctantly, Frenchmen did accept the fact that Germany had become the dominant continental nation, greater in area, population, and industrial output than France.

"Growth politics" complemented "growth economics" in late nineteenth century analyses of the expanding nature of the secular world. Size was made a new criterion of national greatness. Moreover, as the language and thought of Darwinism were distorted into a social outlook, expansion became a condition of political existence, just as it was of biological existence.

"Colonization is for France a matter of life or death." These dramatic words were found in the most famous French imperialist treatise, Paul Leroy-Beaulieu's *De la colonisation chez les peuples mod-*

ernes, first published in 1874. Leroy-Beaulieu went on to state that without colonies France would so diminish in importance as to become a Greece or Romania. Later critics added Switzerland and Belgium to the list—the point being that all these were countries attractive to tourists but not inspiring respect among the great powers. In this argument, imperialism was justified in terms of simple political arithmetic: the greater the territorial sum, the greater the national political factor.

But such vast stretches of territory also provided the particular environment in which a new national spirit would be generated, commentators proclaimed. France's possessions would become a "school of energy," a great out-of-doors in which burnished and lean-muscled young men would find a new vision of France and the determination to follow it. According to this interpretation of empire, the deserts contained more than sand and the savanna more than brush: they were the sources of a particular national mysticism, a valuable element by which to counter the dull domesticity of the bourgeoisie, so well depicted by Daumier and so well described by Balzac.

Novelists, journalists, colonial administrators and polemicists all praised the salubrious effect the new colonial frontier would have on France. The magic word was "action," and it dispelled what were considered the worst social effects of a life of contemplation. The new attitude was not simply colonial, but characteristic of the generation of 1890 which, in the words of the novelist Paul Bourget, wished to escape from the "poison of analysis" that had sickened the previous generation. "All their action was consumed in seeking the reason ... for acting," commented André Tarde and Henri Massis of that generation in a popular work published in 1913 and entitled *Les Jeunes gens d'aujourd'hui*. These authors found that the contemporary generation had retreated from the study and classroom. Instead, "what characterizes their attitude is the *taste for action*." Here was the generation that listened to Bergson, not Descartes, that went on pilgrimages to Chartres with the poet Péguy, and that found, among other activities, *Le Tour de France* an exciting new sporting entertainment.

The colonial world was more than an extension of this robust spirit: it was considered, by its proponents, to be the very source of it. Chailley-Bert treated the matter anthropomorphically when at Bordeaux on March 4, 1903, he lectured that "new blood is infused ... by the young colonies into the old mother country." Most particularly, Africa was deemed the region that best rendered this hematogenic service. "Africa is one of the last sources of national energy," commented the colonial novelist and Saharan officer Ernest Psichari.

Those colonial officers, and there were many, who expressed an interest in national revitalization, agreed with Psichari. Africa was a part of the world that they perceived as being unspoiled, unexplored, unending. The man of action could make his mark there and, in so doing, personally help prepare France for the time when it would again be tested in war.

Of all the colonial figures who upheld this idea, none was more persistent in his assertions of it than Hubert Lyautey, future Resident-General of Morocco. Of aristocratic origin, a monarchist who reconciled himself to the republic and served it well, Lyautey entered the colonial world belatedly (as he lamented), in middle-age. Serving under Gallieni in Indochina and Madagascar, then posted to Algeria, he gained a vast experience which sharpened his generally romantic interpretation of life. His published collection of speeches made during his colonial career is, most appropriately, entitled *Paroles d'action*.

Lyautey's general argument and purpose may by summarized in his own words: he assumed that he had the "social responsibility to snatch this country [France] from decomposition and ruin." What upset him with conditions at home were an inept parliamentary regime, pervasive bureaucratization, and general indolence. And what he thought he and his generation would one day be called upon to stabilize was "this country, so unbalanced between the utopianism of some and the snobbery of others." Liberated, in the colonies, from these conditions, the average Frenchman would again be able to develop his qualities of initiative, endurance, and energetic activity. For Lyautey, there was basically no better or sturdier individual than his own countryman, once he was allowed to be himself. Personal redefinition occurred on the colonial frontier, in that "school of energy" that Lyautey considered Africa and Asia to be. There, a new generation of steeled men would be prepared through whom Lyautey hoped to "establish a continuous circuit, a regenerator of life between the France without and the France within."

None of this language or the thought it expressed is surprising, particularly when considered against the broad industrial fact of the late nineteenth century, that age when the dynamo replaced the Virgin, to borrow from the American author Henry Adams. Energy was a new word, or a word given new meaning, and it was applied to psychological situations as well as to industrial ones. In the colonial African context particularly, it was made to suggest that the land itself galvanized the outsiders who trod upon it. This simple argument about the significance of environmentalism was given succinct, if not elegant, expression by Robert Randau in his novel *Les Explorateurs*

(1909): "The energy of the white man, master of the land and the people, must match the immense energy of the tropics, which roars like the swell of the ocean."

The eternal Sahara, the primordial configurations of the savanna and jungle were challenges which the colonial officer often met with religious awe, and always met with rugged determination—if the literature on the subject is to be believed. Such an idealized view of the great open spaces of the world was a rather new one in French and European thought. Only recently, in Ruskin's time, had the sky, as artistic subject and poetic metaphor, been found. Only since the paintings of Delacroix was the North African countryside romanticized into brute force. Only with the lush paintings of Gauguin and the studied primitivism of Henri Rousseau were the lands beneath the Southern Cross brightly displayed for the imagination of the self-centered Parisian to ponder. And only with the westward expansion of the United States was the frontier converted from a line of political demarcation into a subject of wonder. That Hubert Lyautey referred to North Africa as the French "Far West" illustrates the significance that colonial ideologues attributed to physical space.

All of this may at first glance seem a symbolically cluttered landscape in which to try to situate French nationalism. But the hard political truth was that it could not be situated elsewhere. The European continent, the old French military parade-ground, was closed. Leroy-Beaulieu emphasized this fact before many others resigned themselves to it. In an article appearing in the May 7, 1881, issue of his journal, the *Économiste français*, wherein he was urging the total annexation of Tunisia, he wrote, "All hopes of forceful revenge are vain dreams in face of a Germany of 55,000,000 inhabitants." Alsace and Lorraine were lost, but "Africa is open."

The general French argument for nationalism-*cum*-imperialism was circular and in this respect consistent with energy theories of the day. A traditionally expansive French foreign policy had to be redirected southward, away from Central European affairs. And yet the nation was to find in the colonies the energy by which to face its European problems. The metaphor was electrical, whether intended or not: a closed circuit, or a vast magnetic field.

Of course, the ideology of French imperialism consisted in much more than one great emotional charge. Below the romantic and the metaphysical, there was a solid material base as well. New sources for capital investment, new markets, new sources of raw materials—this economic trinity was revered in France as elsewhere.

Yet historians have been concerned with the historical reality of the French economic situation, which seemed to argue for its exclusion from the major critical theories of capitalist expansion. There appeared to be no economic urgency in France such as had been noticed in Germany or in Britain, where, in Cecil Rhodes' frequently quoted words, "Empire was a bread and butter question." French industrial production was not geared to overseas trade, and what was generally exported were those luxury products with which the name of Paris was associated. Moreover, the most ardent of French imperialists complained that French capital, then in abundance, was hesitant, even "timid" (an often used word at the time), when confronted with the possibility of colonial exportation. It did not move toward the high-return, high-risk colonial markets, where, according to theory, it should have gone, but seemed more comfortably settled in European government bonds, or in stable, rather low-yield markets such as the United States. The general appearance of economic conservatism in imperial enterprise was confirmed by Eugène Étienne, one of the most ardent French imperialists and a wealthy land-holding *colon* from Algeria. As he addressed the 1904 Colonial Congress, he sounded like a *petit bourgeois* from Provence: "We must strive to treat colonial questions ... like fathers of prudent households."

Nevertheless, whatever the degree of reality in such economic conservatism, most French imperialists made the economic argument a categorical imperative. "Colonial policy is the daughter of industrial policy," stated Jules Ferry in a homely expression that caught on. "Without colonies, no exportation," wrote Henri Mager, a lesser-known figure but an equally insistent imperialist. And Étienne, ten years before his prudent-householder speech, argued in a Chamber of Deputies debate in June 1894 that the purpose of empire "was to assure the future of our country in the new continents, to reserve an outlet there for our goods, and also to find raw materials for our industries."

Again, the general argument was made in overtones of fear and concern. The industrial growth of both the United States and Germany greatly bothered the imperial theorists, and so did the European-wide tendency toward protectionism—which tendency, however, had long been official policy in France. This general appraisal of the global economic scene, with a pronounced emphasis on France's relative weakness in overseas markets, led to increasing endorsement of the argument that the colonies were the assured preserves into which industrial goods could be funneled, and from which needed raw materials could be obtained.

Most of the French theoretical structure, like a bungalow in late autumn, still contained the musty odor of its previous occupants. The work of the English school of colonial economists—the writing of Mill, Torrens, and Wakefield—was reinterpreted, adapted, and occasionally criticized in French terms some thirty years after it had initially been posited. This was most evident in the most-cited book of the period.

The seminal study on French colonial economic theory was a prize essay completed in 1870 by a young man of twenty-three, Paul Leroy-Beaulieu's *De la colonisation chez les peuples modernes*. There is a bit of irony found in the fact that the basis for modern French imperialist ideology should have been written so long before the era of the "New Imperialism" and should have been written by an individual whose youthful experience was almost exclusively limited to the reading of secondary sources, most of them of foreign origin.

Although Leroy-Beaulieu's treatise was not published until 1874, it was written in response to a contest sponsored by the Academy of Moral and Political Sciences in 1866. What is important is the fact that the work went through six editions and by 1906 had been expanded into two volumes—an indication that the study, like the subject with which it was concerned, gained in importance and popularity through the years.

De la colonisation is, in format, a standard book of the era, more a descriptive history of national empires than a critical treatment of imperialism in general. Less than one-tenth of the original edition was devoted to theories of overseas expansion and colonial rule, but these pages provide as well argued a summary of the economics of the matter as will be found anywhere in the French literature of the late nineteenth century. And that they constituted the first strong statement on the subject makes them a preface to the economic ideology that would appear in the 1880s.

It is interesting to note that the title page of the book bears a statement from John Stuart Mill's *Political Economy*: " . . . Colonization in the present state of the world is the best affair of business in which the capital of an old and wealthy country can engage." The statement provides one of the major themes developed by Leroy-Beaulieu.

Although he looked at several countries' experience of capital investment and colonization, Leroy-Beaulieu primarily concentrated on Britain and on analyses provided by the British economists Torrens and Wakefield. The question he posed was this: Did the exportation of capital to the colonies have a deleterious effect on the home economy? Was it a drain? His conclusion was strongly negative. An industrial economy, such as Britain's, often produced an excess of goods, which in turn lowered profits and, consequently, the rate of capital investment. A possibility of economic stagnation, of what we today would call a no-growth economy, might thereupon result. Although

Leroy-Beaulieu noted that John Stuart Mill considered this condition a good one, "it simply frightens us," he admitted. However, when capital was exported to the colonies, it resulted in their economic stimulation, and this meant that the colonies would be able to absorb the home country's excessive industrial production, while increasing the general wealth of the world. Therefore, capital so placed abroad "is not lost, but rather multiplied. Everyone profits from its more productive investment in new lands: the colony, the mother country, the entire world, gains an incontestable advantage from it."

In addition to this affirmed economic benefit, there were others, these also relating directly to the nineteenth century market economy. First, colonies provide the commerce of the colonizing country "with a great boost, by stimulating and maintaining its industry and by supplying the inhabitants of the home country—industrialists, workers, consumers—with an increase in profits, salaries, or pleasures." Here, Leroy-Beaulieu was insistent in his dissent from the general argument he found in Adam Smith and Merivale, which stated that of the two particular commercial advantages—increased pleasures and increased home production—the former was the more important. For Leroy-Beaulieu, there was a direct correlation between both; commerce was a two-way street, with new raw materials increasing the European standard of living, and with goods exported to the colonies achieving the same objective.

The arguments arrayed by Leroy-Beaulieu to explain the economic value of colonies were essentially mid-Victorian, cast in the mold of classical free-trade market economics. The constant generation of capital, made possible by its continued reinvestment in new enterprise and economic activity, would assure a healthy market system, and general prosperity for all. Leroy-Beaulieu had a very favorable view of capitalism; he saw no crassly-motivated high financiers at work, as would later Marxist analysts. Nor did he incline toward the fear-economics of later French imperialists, expressed in such statements as "no colonies, no exportation." It is true that the reason why he believed colonial markets to be most secure was that national taste and affection would be transported overseas with the colonist and thus create a preference for home products. Yet his fundamental theme was Mill's statement about colonies being a wise investment for old and wealthy nations. And thus Leroy-Beaulieu's *De la colonisation* was a period piece, even if rather novel in late nineteenth century France.

By the time Leroy-Beaulieu's work was being cited authoritatively—this beginning with the second, 1882, edition—almost all French imperialists were stressing the economic argument.

However, they were more concerned with the question of guaranteed markets than they were with the search for new places for capital investment or raw materials. In this age of intensifying economic competition and concomitant protectionism, the colonial market appeared assured and therefore the major means of relieving domestic production. It was Jules Ferry, Premier in the 1880s and champion of expansion in Tunisia and Indochina, who provided the most insistent argument and the most cited statement: "The protective system is a steam engine without a safety valve unless there is ... a sane and sound colonial policy."

For Ferry, as for others, the stress on the urgent need for markets obscured a fact that was nevertheless soon recognized: the new colonial possessions simply could not perform the functions immediately assigned them by the theorists at home. The economic means by which the indigenous populations might purchase French goods were not available. Before the French market system could expand and flourish overseas, the component parts of the empire had to be developed.

It was Joseph Chailley-Bert who popularized this argument. He insisted that Jules Ferry had confused present realities with future conditions when he proposed that French goods could be exported to the colonies. According to Chailley-Bert, the colonies were only in the "age of agriculture." In a brief but important tract published in 1896 and entitled *Où en est la politique coloniale de la France: L'Âge de l'agriculture*, he declared, "At the beginning of all civilizations is found a pastoral, or agricultural period; the commercial and industrial periods only come later." In thus positing a unilinear system of economic development, he followed in the theoretical tradition of Adam Smith and Karl Marx, both of whom saw economic history as going through distinct stages. But he came particularly close to Marx in his assumption that the various stages might be shortened in duration, but could neither be averted nor bypassed. His conclusion was obvious: because all cultures follow this articulated historical development, the French would have to be patient in their management of the colonies. Not until some time in the future would the vaunted markets be available. This argument soon gained favor, and other theorists began trumpeting that imperialism was, above all, an investment in the nation's economic future.

Yet how that future might best be prepared was a question the imperialists did not avoid. They all recognized one major distinction between the first and second French colonial empires, and this necessarily shaped their deliberations: there were no longer any settlement colonies, Algeria excepted. Situated in climates that were not conducive to European settlement, and characterized by populations that were already large, the new territories were more accurately described as "possessions," not "colonies," most theorists insisted. A particular social relationship necessarily ensued. The European minority would have to enlist the indigenous population in its economic efforts. The frequently suggested social situation was to be that of the colonist as "director" and the indigenous population as "directed." But this relationship was stated more organically and starkly by one author as follows: "The civilized European is the brain that thinks; the native is the arm that performs."

Obviously, such social analysis as this ran counter to the humanistic objectives the French proclaimed as their unique contribution to colonial affairs. Equality of condition, or "assimilation," could not be anticipated in a colonial setting of unequals. Mutual interest, the material benefit to be derived from the economic development of the land, was the new basis for colonial organization. What stands out from the considerable discussion engendered about this subject is the assertion that the French could materially succeed in their colonies only with the support of the populations upon whom they had imposed themselves. This realization explains the great interest in *politique indigène*, in "native policy."

No subject occupied more attention at the several colonial congresses held in the early twentieth century than did this one. General consideration of "native policy" dominated the deliberations of the International Congress of Colonial Sociology, held on the occasion of the Parisian Exhibition of 1900. There gathered was a group of colonial administrators and writers from all over Europe, and they all willingly subscribed to the popular anthropological thinking of the day. Darwinian interpretations of human evolution, persistence of racial distinctions and their cultural implications, climatic effects on personality—these matters were treated to grand academic consideration and to particular suggestions concerning policy. The notion of assimilation was, as might be expected, roundly berated and scratched from the list of *desiderata* in colonial administration. "Native policy" was now required to be congruent with the institutions, beliefs, and wants of the population under colonial rule. As one participant from France stated, "A race can no more be assimilated than metals can be transmuted." Somewhat later, at the closing of the Colonial Congress of 1906, the Minister of Colonies, Georges Leyguès, announced, "The fundamental principal of our colonial policy must be scrupulous respect for the beliefs, customs and traditions of the conquered or protected peoples."

Assembled together, these thoughts formed a new policy, that called "association," which was offered as the best substitute for—antidote to—"assimilation." "Association" never had any of the metaphysical grandeur of assimilation; it was seen as a pragmatic, even an *ad hoc*, response to particular colonial conditions. First provoked by new conditions in Indochina, where cultural traditions and adminis-trative institutions—the mandarinate in particular—imposed a social problem that the French thought could best be resolved by other than direct rule, "association" soon became the acclaimed principle of colonial rule in all parts of the empire. As the French variation of British "indirect rule," it implied an inexpensive and relatively effec-tive means of colonial control, and one eminently suited to the particu-lar economic purposes of modern empire.

Although recognizing these new imperatives, the French could not divest themselves of a sense of cultural superiority. Nor should one expect them to have done so. The ultimate justification for all imperi-alism, in an age of growing political responsibility in Europe, had to be some sort of "mission." How otherwise could Europe's outstand-ing republic, proudly resting on the tradition of the great Revolution of 1789 and the political liberty that it ideologically professed, justify acts of military domination? France, declared the critics of "assimila-tion," too enthusiastically plays the role of schoolteacher to the world. And yet Chailley-Bert, among the most ardent supporters of "associa-tion," in 1908 said, without worry over contradiction, "Today we have decided to consider the natives as pupils whom we must protect, materially at first, morally afterwards . . . ." Or, to put the matter of "native policy" at its theoretically most mixed, turn to the words of the Minister of Colonies, Paul Deschanel, as he addressed the French Colonial Congress of 1907: "To elevate, civilize the native, to associ-ate him with our program of colonization, to make him a beneficiary of his own land, there is our program."

The historical truth seems to be that, regardless of theoretical variations or proposed policy changes, the basic objective found in French imperialist ideology remained the *mission civilisatrice*. As justification and ideal, it served well a nation that saw as its historical duty the illumination of reason and the introduction of fraternity around the world.

In contrast with this well-polished purpose, which certainly gave a respectable patina to colonial domination, there was the argument that colonial domination was "natural." This was, of course, the French variant of biological struggle and natural competition. Although the French, unlike the Germans, Americans, and British, mustered no great theorists or exponents on this subject, they had their own contingent of "brutalists" who argued that all expansion was ineluctable, a fundamentally natural, but violent, form of growth.

"The struggle for existence is the natural and permanent condition of the human race, as it is for animal species," commented Gustave Le Bon in his *Les Premières civilisations*, published in the centennial year of the French Revolution. Certainly the statement could never pass for original or unusual, but it served to remind imperialists that fraternity under such conditions was not possible. Even though Le Bon himself travelled in the colonial world, he was best known for his exploratory theories on crowd psychology and for his grand and futile efforts to map out the psychological development of mankind. It was, therefore, as a general theorist that he influenced French imperialist thinking, particularly in its consideration of "native policy."

"Force," argued Le Bon, "is the true natural law, the one that dominates the entire history of humanity." From this statement to the epigram "Without force, no colonization" was no great intellectual leap forward. The latter comment was made by Charles Régismanset in his brief but "forceful" *Essai sur la colonisation*, published in 1906. Régismanset was not one of the major French colonial thinkers, and this particular work was not prominently displayed on the library shelves of the French colonial societies. But it did succinctly express the thought that was to be expounded in the most significant imperialist treatise published in the prewar era, save, of course, the work by Leroy-Beaulieu. Jules Harmand's *Domination et colonisation* has attained the status of a minor classic, nearly as often quoted now in historical assessments as it was read then.

Published in 1910, the study was a distillation of Harmand's personal experiences as physician and *commissaire-général* in Tonkin in the early 1870s, and his general reading on the subject of imperialism. The theoretical basis of his argument was clearly derivative, a combination of arguments made by men such as Le Bon with a popular interpretation of Nietzsche's will-to-power. As he reviewed the history of humanity, he argued that expansion was a "fatal obligation" imposed by the very nature of human existence: one must conquer or die. Even though Harmand willingly admitted that conquests were immoral, they were in a more basic sense inevitable, the effect of the latter argument tending to neutralize the former.

The important point Harmand wished to make, however, was this: colonial domination was achieved and could be maintained only by force. The conqueror therefore could never expect freely-given support from the peoples he ruled, nor could he expect to live in other than an unequal social relationship. Under no conditions would foreign domination be accepted; it had to be imposed. Conquest by the sword, he concluded, must be maintained by the sword. "This is the punishment for [the conqueror's] violence, the stain of blood which nothing can eradicate from his hands."

Because of these conditions, Harmand insisted that assimilation could never work. The government of the conqueror was necessarily despotic, with the most generous role that the conqueror could play being that of *bon tyran*, charitable but firm. In light of these less then amicable social conditions, Harmand insisted that France's colonial possessions be described as they in fact were: "dominations."

However, Harmand argued that something good could come from all of this. Conquest might be "authorized" by the conqueror's superiority, he stated, and the act may be "excused" by necessity, but the ensuing relationship must also be developed according to mutual advantage. There were economic benefits which the indigenous population, as well as the colonial power, should obtain. Because any economic development of France's "dominations" in tropical zones would depend on the collaboration of the indigenous population, the more the latter were given the opportunity to benefit materially, the more tolerable the situation would be. The policy that could achieve this was, according to Harmand, that of "association."

Regardless of the intellectual tack taken, either one in which "respect" for local institutions was requested, or one in which "force" required inequality, turn-of-the-century theorists in general subscribed to the practical policy of "association" and therefore rejected the more abstract concept of "assimilation."

The debate over "native policy" was an integral part of French imperialist ideology. Whether expansion was to revitalize the nation, enrich it, or politically strengthen it, this would have to be done through the use of the conquered populations. To employ military terms, the issue was social mobilization to enhance the national strategies of France.

But, for all that, the French produced no "grand plan" or grand criticism of imperialism. Most of the important writings consisted in brief journal or newspaper articles, and speeches in parliament or before public gatherings. There was no eminent volume that has held historical attention, like the Englishman J. A. Hobson's *Imperialism, A Study*, or the American Josiah Strong's *Our Country*. Harmand's study was the most imaginative, and Leroy-Beaulieu's was the most detailed, but neither provided the major synthesis that might have been expected. If there was a grandly probing study that treated imperialism both as a category of thought and a condition of human existence, it was Ernest Seillière's three-volume work *La Philosophie de l'impérialisme*, which appeared between 1903 and 1907. But, however provocative it was, the work was not even mentioned by the proponents of imperialism, and today it retains significance only as a preface of sorts to Oswald Spenger's *Decline of the West*.

It may indeed be the fact, as some historians have argued, that Jules Ferry brought the disparate elements of imperialist ideology together in his general thinking, if not in any one of his speeches in particular. He alighted, at one time or another, on each of the points that had been made by the theorists. He spoke of the material and the patriotic, of the strategic and the political. Nothing eluded his attention, but his chief concern was with the economics of expansion in an industrial age. It was during his two Premierships, 1881 and 1883–5, that Tunisia was seized and serious military operations in the Tonkin area of Indochina were endorsed. The latter activity brusquely toppled Ferry, who was derisively hooted as "Le Tonkinois" by a nation doubtful of military adventure. Still, in his day he was also acclaimed as the originator of French colonial expansion, an "honor" he has still retained, although not without question. By the time, 1890, that he published his extensive preface to a volume of documents entitled *Tonkin et la mère-patrie*, a sort of justification of his previous activity in government, the imperial idea was successfully making its way among the French population. And, although that preface stands as the best economic justification for imperialism since Leroy-Beaulieu first broached the subject, its importance is as a summary statement, not as a new or larger synthesis.

By 1900, all French imperialists were employing the same basic arguments with little variation in analysis or expression: civilizing mission, economic necessity, reinforced political power. This ideological tripod was one upon which rested the colonial policy of almost every nation then seeking places near the setting sun. Nevertheless, what popular appeal empire had in France at the turn of the century was derived from arguments concerning nationalism.

The myth of the hexagon of French power and influence in the world had been accepted as a schoolboy's truism. By geographical location, by historical development, and, therefore, by destiny, France had to play a major role in world affairs. Such was the national categorical imperative. "France cannot be France without greatness," asserted General De Gaulle in the introductory lines of his war *Mémoires*.

The phrase *La Plus Grande France*, which Chailley-Bert popularized at the turn of the century, appropriately summarized this long-enduring sentiment. As in the century of Louis le Grand, as in the era of Napoleon's "Grand Empire," France again, but now under republican auspices, stood in the forefront of nations. Yet the comparative adjective "greater," in Chailley-Bert's phrase, said something else also. It was actually derived from Sir Charles Dilke's *Greater Britain*, published in 1869, after that author had ventured through the various English-speaking portions of the world. What then impressed Dilke was the extensiveness and the persistence of British civilization, a global accomplishment of which the British could justifiably be proud, he thought. The French, heretofore both annoyed and awed by the multicontinental dimensions of the island kingdom, were now able to return in spirit Dilke's pride. They joyously spoke of new worlds aborning in which songs of praise would be sung in French— or on behalf of the French, if the "natives" had not yet learned the newly imported language.

La Plus Grande France was therefore more than a phrase that had rhetorical appeal at the turn of the century: it also represented a new reality. France had gone overseas.

Chapter Three

The Definition of Empire

Any unity that the theorists at home initially perceived in the new empire was of their own imagination, an ideal. Abroad, the territories that were nominally French—so inscribed on maps and through treaties—exhibited the variety of conditions that particular climate, economic organization, and cultural development necessarily imposed. Yet, even when they spoke patriotically of "Overseas France," most of the imperialists had no serious intention of treating the many possessions as a single *bloc*; on the contrary, they recognized the need for flexibility, ingenuity, and realism in colonial administration. Quite simply, the lack of capital, colonists, and large numbers of troops meant that colonial rule would, *de facto*, rest on some sort of collaboration with, therefore adjustment to, the local social and political order. The French were soon to learn, as did every other European colonial power, that the grand dreams of empire were beyond the collective abilities and desires of late nineteenth century nations. As the British so aptly put it at the time, what was really wanted was empire "on the cheap," an activity that cost little in gold, lives, and effort.

Defining then organizing the newly-created French colonial world did, however, involve the talents and energies of a small number of dedicated men. They immediately knew that the most pressing problem was "pacification," a nineteenth century euphemism for military suppression. The difference between what historians have called "paper" annexation and annexation-in-fact was a vast one. Occupation of the littoral region, as in Algeria, or negotiation with the local ruler, as in Tunisia or Equatorial Africa, did not automatically assure widespread acceptance of the new French presence. Regional pockets of resistance, often formed around the person of a dynamic leader, made early appearances. Whether these become anachronistic when described as part of "national liberation movements" is not of great consequence to the historical situation of the time. From the colonial perspective, they were either annoying or threatening problems to French rule and therefore had to be extirpated. But to extirpate them the French military forces, usually very small in proportion to the populations they were attempting to subdue, found it necessary to depend on local collaboration. This very basic condition was most influential in the formation of a new "native policy" and clearly suggested that the actuality of the colonial situation predated and preformed the theoretical explanations of it.

One generalization therefore stands out along all the historical boundaries of the incipient empire: it was the military that assured the French "colonial peace," and did so in both military and political terms. In fact, the theoretically most original of French colonial officers, and one of the most important of them, General Joseph Gallieni (best remembered in the popular mind for his imaginative use of Parisian taxis, to rush troops into the first Battle of the Marne), remarked early in his career that military and political policy went hand-in-hand. In his "Instructions to the Civilian Administrators and Military Chiefs in the Field," written in 1896 during the conquest of Madagascar, Gallieni put it this way: "It is the combined action of politics and force which should result in the pacification of the country and the rudimentary organization that it will first have."

Yet, in stating this, Gallieni was not speaking either in a new tone or on a new subject in matters of French colonial practice. In the years in which the French colonial empire was being defined, a rather amazing dynasty of military leadership was created, each major officer recognizing the efforts of his predecessor and, generally, formulating his own military policy on that pursued before him. Thomas Bugeaud, Louis Faidherbe, Joseph Gallieni, and Hubert Lyautey are the names of the four masters of colonial warfare and occupation. They also provide an easily appreciated continuity of military personality in French imperial history. Bugeaud waged his form of colonial war in Algeria in 1836–7 and 1841–7. Faidherbe served in Algeria in 1843–6 and again in 1849–52, and while there personally observed, participated in, and appreciated Bugeaud's techniques. From 1854 to 1861 and from 1863 to 1864, he was military commander in Senegal, where he modified and improved some of the military techniques of administration that he had learnt in Algeria, and the great success of his methods led Gallieni, who first served in Senegal in 1879, to build upon them. In 1892 Gallieni was posted to Indochina, where the latest and newest of the significant colonial officers, Hubert Lyautey, first served under him in 1894; later he followed Gallieni to Madagascar, where he was his subordinate from 1897 to 1902. In 1912, Lyautey reached his pinnacle of fame and power by becoming Resident-General in Morocco, which post he held, with one brief change, until 1925. So successful did his policy there appear, that French colonial administrators took him as the model of an outstanding administrator.

What is of particular concern here, however, is not the seemingly simple chain of cause and effect in the military career of this grand quadrumvirate, but the policy they established and defended. It was not of whole cloth, but a patchwork, the clear pattern of which did not become discernible until towards the end of the nineteenth century, when Gallieni's "methods" were widely praised by colonial officers in the field and theorists at home.

Before all stood the aging but firm figure of Marshal Thomas Bugeaud, Duke of Isly, farmer and peasant at heart, militarist and monarchist by profession and social leaning. Bugeaud had the sharp countenance of a bird of prey, his nose aquiline, as with the conquerors of old. He may have been a "Cato the Elder who knew no Latin," as one French historian has described him, but he was, by all testimony, a rude individual whose language and personal interests better complemented those of his common soldiers than those of his aristocratic officers.

More important, Bugeaud was at best a reluctant imperialist. And, more precisely, he initially opposed the French occupation of Algeria and said as much to Adolphe Thiers in 1836, when the latter was enjoying one of his several moments at the helm of the French ship of state. "Algiers is worth absolutely nothing, either as a land to cultivate or as a field in which to make war," said Bugeaud with his usual peremptoriness.

And yet, from 1841 to 1847, he maneuvered militarily in Algeria and sent regular dispatches home and to his officers, describing the manner in which the land could best be colonized. His actions were not, however, regarded with enthusiasm, either then or later. Of the quadrumvirate, Bugeaud is and has remained the most controversial, appearing to some critics as more an Attila in French uniform than a French soldier enrobed in the best of Cartesian thought.

Bugeaud came to the Algerian colonial scene because military matters were not going well there, and his monarch, King Louis-Philippe, longed for a little cloud of glory on which to waft his sons to political success. That Bugeaud was not a man to share the fluff of glory, any more than to negotiate his military policies with ministers at home or commanders in the field, was something that the

Bourgeois King had yet to learn. By 1847, when Bugeaud retired to his farm in the Dordogne region, he left behind an Algeria that was militarily dominated and an opposition at home that was militantly organized.

Bugeaud's policy and practice were as simply joined as they were brutally enacted. He believed that military colonization—both conquest and administrative organization thereafter—was the only method that assured France success. His contempt for the civilian politicians at home and for most of the civilian settlers and administrators he was encountering in Algeria was quite notorious. But he got on nearly as badly with his military subordinates, berating them in dispatches and in his correspondence. One of the king's sons, the Duke of Aumale, referred to Bugeaud as a "crude corporal"—not the only time in European history that well-placed aristocrats have employed such a term.

But what did Bugeaud do besides easily provoke commentary from his associates? Most significantly, he turned the French occupation of Algeria from a restricted, coastal affair into an all-out war for the hinterland. The territorial creation of modern Algeria, as both colony and nation, was more the work of Bugeaud than of anyone else. This he did in opposition to the similar, but more noble, intentions expressed by Abd-el-Kader, a religious figure who wrought near-wonders politically in the western reaches of Algeria. Leader of a *jihad* (holy war) against the infidels and the wayward within Algeria, Abd-el-Kader took the title of Caliph, suggesting the combined religious and secular authority he claimed as his own and which, it is important to stress, was equally given him by his followers. By the time Bugeaud appeared on the scene, Kader had amassed a large land empire, but one away from the French on the coast—because, as he said, he did not intend to rule the sea. However, "border conflicts," harassment of French outposts in the province of Oran, but particularly the cutting off of the camp at Tafna, near the city of Oran, brought the French into Kader's sphere.

Bugeaud's first African assignment, on his arrival in Algeria in 1836, was to relieve this situation. When he arrived, he brought with him a varied military experience acquired under Napoleon. What he remembered most and also adapted to the present military conditions was his activity during Napoleon's invasion of Spain, where the guerrilla warfare—coined in name and practice at that time by the Spanish—had made it necessary to revise French tactics. Mobility, swift action made possible by reducing the size of the supply train and the amount of equipment used by the troops, and harsh treatment of the enemy and his civilians were the lessons Bugeaud then used. Had

Goya been a resident of Algeria in the 1830s, he probably would have painted scenes of horror not much different from those he actually painted, as a resident of Spain in the 1800s.

What Bugeaud has been condemned for most is his policy of the "razzia"—the military destruction of population, property, and land—which he considered necessary in order to get at the "interests" of the inhabitants. In Europe the same end could have been achieved by the seizure of a city or of commerce, but in Algeria, as an essentially nomadic and rural land, he argued, the only way the population could have its "interests" gravely affected was by the destruction of its economic base: hence crops were burned, livestock was seized, residences were destroyed, and families were dispersed. These acts of destruction were effected by large but highly mobile columns of soldiers, which struck and then withdrew.

Clearly, what Bugeaud had in mind was the military subjugation of the country. His family device was "by the sword and with the plough." In Algeria, the second means came later and, in Bugeaud's case, much less successfully.

Bugeaud's "native policy" was formed not as a result of contempt or respect for the people he militarily conquered, but out of expediency. Rather than impose French institutions, he thought the best method of control would be to leave as much authority as possible in the hands of traditional rulers, and to disturb the ways of the people as little as the imposition of French rule required. But, by an ordinance of April 15, 1845, introduced by the home government and not because of any wishes of Bugeaud, the country's French settler population was divided into three units of administration. In the French settled areas along the coast, the administration was civilian and drawn along French metropolitan lines, structured in what were called *communes de pleine exercice*. Where Algerians and French lived in a less satisfactory demographic relationship, a "mixed" military–civilian administration was created. And, finally, in the vast, uncolonized region of the Algerian hinterland, there was only a military regime.

It was in this last administrative unit that Bugeaud's "native policy" was imposed. He reinstituted and developed into a major element of administrative control the "Arab bureaux." In each of the military regions Bugeaud established a bureau, with, at its head, a military officer schooled in Algerian ways, appreciative of Islam, and with a knowledge of Arabic. His job was to advise the military on Arab matters, and to act as mediator between the French and the local population in an effort to influence the local leaders. This primitive example of "indirect rule" met with initial success, but by mid-century the personnel of the Arab bureaux were abusing their authority and appearing more as satraps in the new imperial system than as negotiators.

Even less successful than this agency was Bugeaud's attempt at military colonization in the formal sense of the phrase. He desired to retire campaign soldiers to the Algerian countryside and there to set them up as farmers, to develop the land. It was not, as he was careful to say, that he opposed civilian colonization, but that ex-military personnel could also serve as part of a militia, quickly assembled in case of revolt. Here again, Bugeaud revealed his assessment of the Arabs as warlike peoples, difficult to rule by accepted European methods.

Lastly, Bugeaud, like his successors, was a *constructeur* of sorts. He saw the need for public works and urged that the military be involved in their creation. In a circular dated November 15, 1844, he wrote, "One of the best methods by which to accustom the Arabs to our domination is to favor their interests in every way possible, but especially by public works, which will give them commercial facilities or increase their agricultural wealth and daily comforts."

Bugeaud's colonial plans were no more easily implemented than his defeat of Abd-el-Kader was assured. The Caliph proved to be a resilient and resourceful foe, whose religious fervor and mobile strategy matched Bugeaud's determination. Bugeaud's military campaign of 1842 did effectively destroy Kader's empire, but not until 1847 was the Caliph finally captured and exiled. In the same year Bugeaud was retired, leaving behind an Algeria that was not converted to civilian rule until 1879.

In broad terms, Bugeaud contributed significantly to French colonial method and practice. First, he left a strong military imprint on the enterprise, carried from Algeria to West Africa and on to Indochina. Secondly, he argued and demonstrated the need for accommodation to the local culture in order to maintain the "colonial peace." While his system of Arab bureaux was not exported, his insistence on personnel who knew and could work well in the context of the local culture was widely followed. Thirdly, his perception of a need to correlate military conquest and political control was reflected elsewhere. As he wrote to his officers in a circular dated September 17, 1844, "After conquest, the first task, as it is also the primary interest of the conqueror, is to govern the defeated people well, with politics and basic humanity equally commanding the conqueror's attention." But, as subsequent critics have argued, Bugeaud's policy was excessively harsh, almost contradictory. He first destroyed the land that he later wished to reorganize. "Basic humanity" was not a quality he carried in his military knapsack. Finally, the very harshness of Bugeaud's military policy, the continuing opposition to the man and his plans, as expressed in parliament, and the series of insurrections that afflicted French colonial rule in Algeria until the third quarter of the nineteenth century stood as reminders that Bugeaud was not the hero that Faidherbe, Gallieni and Lyautey were considered to be.

Bugeaud's lineal successor in the colonial empire was Louis Faidherbe, who made his mark and acquired his historical significance far south of the Algerian border, in West Africa. However, Faidherbe bore little resemblance to Bugeaud, in background, appearance, or personality. A republican by persuasion, a bourgeois by birth, and a quiet, if autocratic, man by temperament, his outward bearing was anything but aristocratic. Narrow-shouldered and slightly built, his eyes hidden behind steel-rimmed glasses, he looked more a Dickensian clerk than a builder of empire. But the latter was his function. Playing a part similar to that that Bugeaud had played in Algeria, he extended Senegal from a few small coastal stations into an ill-defined colony extending into the hinterland of the Upper Niger.

Faidherbe profited from his six years' service in Algeria, but in what manner is still an issue of historical debate. He fought in the razzias, had mixed feelings about the Arabs as a people, but gained an appreciation of Islam as a cultural force. The military approach to colonization was one he learned in Algeria and brought with him to Senegal. Nevertheless, he recognized that the situation in Senegal was necessarily different from that in Algeria. Indeed, so did the French Ministry of the Navy, which stated in a document of 1859, "Nothing similar to Algeria could be undertaken in Senegal." Although Faidherbe was in favor of European settlement, he saw that the French had little interest in becoming colonists (emigration to Algeria had been small) and concluded that Senegal would have to be a territory administered by the French, not settled by them. It is to Faidherbe's credit and was an expression of his realism that he recognized that Senegal was in fact a "possession," not a colony.

The process of establishing French control of this possession was one he entered into with military flair and diplomatic skill. His policy of pacification involved not only the rendition of very immediate opposition, such as the Moors who controlled the left bank of the Senegal River, but also the extensive and long military campaign he waged against El-Hadj Omar, who himself was leading a *jihad* among the peoples of the Upper Niger and whose activities, moreover, reminded the French of those of Abd-el-Kader in Algeria. After the defeat of the Moors, Faidherbe showed himself to be a wise peacemaker, for the treaties he signed with them were intentionally generous, so as to reduce the threat of retaliation, and so allow him greater freedom of action.

Against El-Hadj Omar the campaign was more severe, but by 1863 the jihadic empire had been pushed back, and, at the time of Omar's death, in 1864, it was in a state of disorganization. Yet to suggest that Faidherbe had defeated the Islamic forces would be to distort history: they were severely repelled but returned to cause the French further headaches, particularly in the late 1870s. Meantime, Faidherbe worked to make the territory into which he was penetrating militarily stable. His own design for a local *pax colonia* was described in a striking set of orders given to naval lieutenant Mage, who was charged with an embassy to El-Hadj Omar in June 1863. Therein Faidherbe explained that he wished to construct a line of military posts that "would serve as places for storing merchandise and products as well as points of protection for caravans" and so provide a "commercial avenue between Senegal and the Upper Niger." In Faidherbe's scheme, military expansion had commercial objectives.

Of equal importance at the time and of greater historical interest was the policy Faidherbe adopted toward the local populations. Most French commentators laud Faidherbe for his humanitarian interest in black Africans. In 1858, when the home government was considering forcibly taking Senegalese and shipping them off to plantations in the Antilles, he rather dramatically threatened to resign. The government relented and Faidherbe stayed on. In a note written about the same time to his military associates in Senegal, Faidherbe simply defined his policy: "Because of the differences in race and religion, it is best to let the [local populations] regulate their own affairs as much as possible."

Yet the respect he suggested was also matched by his own efforts at change. He joined colonization with civilization, in the words of one French historian. More particularly, he attempted by means of education to convert the Senegalese populations to French ways. First, he established a series of Franco-Moslem schools in which children were taught French and other subjects, all non-religious. Then in 1855 he founded the "School of Hostages", for the purpose of training as interpreters and future colonial administrators the young men held as a gage to insure that local rulers would maintain their treaty arrangements with the French. The name of this school was soon changed to the "School for the Sons of Chiefs and Interpreters," and under the new guise lasted until 1871, when it was abolished. In 1857 Faidherbe began the Tirailleurs Sénéglais, as a regular unit of his colonial forces. They were outfitted and trained in French fashion, and provided the nucleus for later, more extensive use of "native troops."

Perhaps his most lasting influence on Senegalese colonial affairs was the military gridwork he imposed on the land. Here his Algerian experience stood before his imagination. "In Algeria and Senegal the aim is the same," he wrote, "the difficulties are analogous—the means to reach them the same." Faidherbe arranged the country in military units: *arrondissements*, which were each governed by a *commandant*; and the smaller *cercles*. To begin with, the *cercle* was placed under the jurisdiction of an indigenous ruler, but later its organization was modified so that a French officer held the most effective power. This new *commandant de cercle* became and remained until the end of the French colonial experience in West Africa the basic colonial official, resembling in principle, if not in fact, the British district officer.

Enthusiastically respected by French historians living in the era of the Third Republic, more critically evaluated by recent historians, Faidherbe remains the first historical example of the modern French colonial administrator, working with and through local institutions, cautious in his imposition of French methods, experimental and realistic in his general approach. That he believed Western civilization to be superior to African culture cannot be denied. In his letter of proposed resignation in 1858, he referred to the black Africans as "races little favored by nature from the point of view of human perfectability." But he also recognized the fact that the economic development of the colonial territories, an objective he considered imperative, rested on cooperation with and respect from the indigenous peoples. This was the solid base of his own "native policy," what Georges Hardy, the French biographer of Faidherbe, referred to as his "policy of association."

The combined activity of military conquest and political reform that Faidherbe worked in Senegal was elaborated upon and elevated to doctrine by Joseph Gallieni.

Almost literally following in Faidherbe's footsteps, Gallieni arrived in West Africa in 1879, at the outset of his colonial career, to take up his first major military assignment. He was charged with responsibility for obtaining a treaty from Ahmadou Segou, son of and successor to El-Hadj Omar—another interesting political link in the succession of French colonial dynasties. The French were anxious to begin construction of a railroad—to drain the riches of the interior to the coast, or so they hoped—and to this end wished to establish a protectorate over those of Ahmadou's territories through which the railroad would have to pass, and to obtain exclusive trade rights in the area. Gallieni was politically held off by Ahmadou, then struggling to maintain his hold over the empire that his father had created and which his relatives now coveted. After a delay of nearly a year, he signed a treaty that the French said assured a protectorate, but that Ahmadou insisted concerned only trade. Such were the pressing difficulties created by the subtle differences of meaning inevitable in dual-language treaties, and the gross differences of diplomatic intention.

By 1886 Gallieni's career had gone from negotiation to command, with his assumption of military leadership of the Upper Niger region, into which the French had recently moved. Through his efforts in the field, the French Empire was further extended, into the territory later known as the French Sudan, with its capital at Bamako.

From his African service, Gallieni gained an appreciation of Faidherbe's methods, and an understanding of the particular need to adjust to the political and cultural situation in which the peoples encountered lived. What was required he called a *politique des races*: political flexibility in varying colonial situations and, most particularly, fitting the method to the needs of the locale.

From Africa Gallieni went to Indochina, where, owing to Vietnamese resistance supported by Chinese irregulars and pirate groups, the most famous of which was the "Black Flags," the northern provinces of Tonkin were in a state of turbulence. It was in Tonkin that Gallieni's colonial talent was first well displayed and to the admiration of his not-so-young subordinate Hubert Lyautey, who there, at the age of thirty-nine, was really only just beginning to experience the colonial life. "Vive la méthode Gallieni!" Lyautey then exclaimed. And he would repeat himself more than once, even commenting directly to Gallieni in Madagascar, "I regard myself as the apostle of your ideas, the standard-bearer of your method . . . ."

What was Gallieni doing that garnered such admiration? In his Tonkin activities, he pursued a method that he labelled a *tache d'huile*, a stain of oil. The meaning of the "stain" is this: colonial soldiers were not to conquer by devastation and destruction, but to subdue by well-considered occupation of the land. But Lyautey explained it more effectively in a letter from Hanoi, dated February 5, 1895, and addressed to his brother. "To this military activity," he wrote, "Gallieni adds a simultaneous effort at organization—roads, telegraphs, markets, European and native businesses, of the sort to assure that along with pacification there advances, like a stain of oil, a large perimeter of civilization. . . . It's improved Bugeaud."

Later critics would argue, more correctly, that, by being an effective correlation of military and political activity, Gallieni's method was quite different from Bugeaud's. Gallieni did not destroy in order to build, but attempted to build as he conquered.

His approach became raised to the level of theory, and, soon after, doctrine, when he was assigned to Madagascar, as confused and unsettled colonial terrain as the French encountered. Not only was there still Anglo-French rivalry there, dating from missionary activities in the middle of the century, but in addition the island's

internal politics were chaotic. The Merina monarchy had become the
dominant force, in part through earlier French encouragement. But
the lack of a particular hegemony over the island and the severe
opposition of other island groups to the Merina meant that the pros-
pect of a *pax colonia* was still remote.

With his customary dispatch, Gallieni reviewed and carefully
weighed the situation and then effectively combined the two elements
of his colonial practice: the *politique des races* and the *tache d'huile*. By the
time he left Madagascar in 1905, the populations had been subdued,
the island was reasonably well administered and on its way to
economic development. In the same period Gallieni combined action
with contemplation and thereby produced a series of declarations and
other writings which served French colonial warfare in much the same
way as Napoleon's dispatches had served French European warfare.

Gallieni devised French "native policy" more effectively and
influentially than anyone else. Some historians have even argued that
modern French colonial administration began with Gallieni's regime
on Madagascar. If the claim is too much, there is still no doubt that
Gallieni played a distinctive role in the development of French colonial
theory.

The essence of his thought is as follows. First, he insisted that
military and political action were interrelated and should occur simultaneously. Secondly, as the occupation forces moved into a new
territory, they should impress the local population with their intention
to stay and to develop the region. He therefore urged that the military
construct permanent posts or forts, and then establish a market near
them, in order to stimulate trade and peaceful contact. This was the
tache d'huile, which Gallieni stated meant that "territory in front is won
only after that behind has been completely organized." Thirdly, Gallieni insisted upon flexibility and accommodation. "The administrative organization of a new country must be perfectly in harmony with
its resources, its configuration, the general outlook of its inhabitants,
and the proposed objective." So he stated in his famous Instructions of
May 22, 1898.

Looking over his career from his service on the Niger to his service
in Madagascar, Gallieni saw continuity in his development of a colonial policy; but this continuity also meant discontinuity in traditional
French colonial theory. No one was more ardently opposed to assimilation, or more enthusiastically in favor of association, than he.

As Gallieni worked and acted, his admiring subordinate, Hubert
Lyautey, avidly learned. His first lesson, which he later recalled, was
pleasantly dramatic. During his first evening with Gallieni, Lyautey
was asked by the Colonel if he had brought any good theoretical

studies with him. Lyautey replied that he had, and Gallieni then asked if he might see them. When Lyautey produced a handful of official military manuals, Gallieni took them, carefully tied them together in a neat bundle, and then placed the item in a sideboard. As Lyautey watched, Gallieni remarked, "You will do me the great favor of leaving all of that here and forgetting it. Nothing in these manuals is relevant to the sort of war and other activities we engage in here."

There is no doubt whatsoever that Lyautey's feelings, hopes, and ideas were given structure by Gallieni in his dual capacity of individual and colonial practitioner. The student perhaps excelled the teacher.

Lyautey was an imperialist of the proconsular school. He is best contrasted with Faidherbe and even Bugeaud. A man of elegant ways, cultural sensitivity, romantic feelings, and grand dreams, he certainly belonged outside the continental confines of Third Republic France. In Morocco, where he practiced his *métier* with true flair, he could appear seated on a white horse and with a black burnous gracefully draped over his army uniform, his persona equal to that of the Sultan, or—should we say it?—the T. E. Lawrence of Arabian myth.

Both in Indochina and in Madagascar, Lyautey served as Gallieni's subordinate, but the relationship between the men was that of comradeship, not military fastidiousness. Lyautey's correspondence clearly indicates his profound respect for Gallieni as soldier and administrator. Lyautey's colonial policy was a respectful and intelligent adaptation of what he learned from and with Gallieni. He put it all to good advantage in his principal colonial assignment.

Morocco, one of the most attractive colonial possessions acquired by France, was also the last major addition to the French Empire. The countryside, the people, and the land's rich culture were combined in a unique way. And so were the politics, as confused internally as could be imagined and as aggravated externally as turn-of-the-century European relations would allow. France, Germany, Britain, and Spain were all "interested parties" where the well-being, or wealth, of the Cherifian Empire was concerned. Like his confrere in Tunisia, the Sultan had become indebted to European moneylenders, while rival factions created an internal military turbulence that European imperialists viewed hopefully.

On the diplomatic level, two Moroccan crises preceded Lyautey's arrival, both involving France and Germany, and seeming to threaten war, as each nation maneuvered for power and influence. The diplomatic resolution of the second crisis, in 1911, paved the way for French hegemony. Border disputes on the Algerian–Moroccan frontier, and approaching internal anarchy—French conveniences as much as Moroccan problems—provided the necessary excuse. The French military occupation was accepted by the Sultan and acquiesced in by the European powers. On paper and in ceremony, France added another unit to its extensive North African empire.

Lyautey came to Morocco after brief service in France and then Algeria. The internal military disorder of Morocco led the French government away from consideration of a civilian administrator and, in part on the recommendation of Gallieni, the new assignment was offered to Lyautey. The Premier at the time, Raymond Poincaré, informed the French parliament that "the name of General Lyautey is in itself the equivalent of a complete colonial program."

That program began with "pacification," which for once was meant in something other than a euphemistic sense. Lyautey reversed the proposition of Bugeaud by insisting that political action should precede and, where possible, preclude military action. In a famous line, he insisted that "it was necessary to display force in order to avoid its use." Thus the semblance of superior military power might be enough to convince the enemy to surrender. True, in some instances this worked, but Lyautey subdued Morocco not in a few months or a few years. The fact is, Morocco did not arrive at a state of internal peace until 1934. Lyautey recognized the incredible nature of this problem when he remarked in his New Year's Day reception for the French community in Rabat in 1920, "It is a situation without precedent and quite paradoxical to witness a country, a third of which . . . still remains to be conquered . . . yet where the colonializing activity is developing with an intensity and rapidity never seen elsewhere."

Throughout the years during which he was in charge in Morocco, he pursued his policy of caution and care in military operations. Like Gallieni, he knew the importance of securing the rear, of making the French presence seem both permanent and beneficial. Next to the fort should appear the market-place, he said, to stimulate both trade and better relations between French and Moroccans. In the unsubdued regions where colonial warfare took place, he used swiftly-moving columns, capable of enveloping the enemy and denying him retreat. And, in the Gallieni manner, he thought it wise to construct strong forts, to demonstrate the seriousness of French intentions as well as to secure military ascendancy.

Yet the truth of the matter is that Lyautey's real concern was not with conquest but with preservation. He wished to administer Morocco, strengthen it along its own lines of development, not convert it. He was therefore given to stressing the point that Morocco was not a colony like Algeria, but an integral society, however disarrayed, that France was charged with reaffirming and guiding. "While in other parts of North Africa, we only found social debris," he stated in 1922, "here ... we have found a constituted empire, and with it a beautiful and great civilization.... A remarkable Morocco can be created, one that will remain Moroccan and Islamic." It was his arabophilia, often noted, that so well suited Lyautey to his post but it also incurred the displeasure of politicians at home who wished Morocco to become French in economic and political purpose.

Under these circumstances, and in light of his previous experiences, it is not surprising to find that Lyautey pursued a policy of association. As he said in Casablanca in 1924, "This agreeable and frank association of the two races is the best and surest guarantee of the future in Morocco." For Lyautey, the relationship was one of parallel structure, with the French being as unobtrusive as possible, and the traditional Moroccan authorities continuing to function as before, but under French direction. In outward appearances, certainly, and in the depths of Lyautey's intentions, the Cherifian government continued as before, the imperial flag prominently displayed, and Lyautey and his officers discreetly out of sight when the new Sultan, Moulay Youssef, made his tour of the major Moroccan cities in 1912. That Moslem prayers were offered for Lyautey's well-being when, years later, he was suffering through a liver infection is proof enough that he had satisfied his own objectives.

Early in October 1925 Lyautey sailed for home, and his colonial career was ended. It had been in June 1836 that Bugeaud first sailed for Algeria. In a little less than 100 years, the colonial quadrumvirate of Bugeaud, Faidherbe, Gallieni and Lyautey had defined and indelibly marked the colonial policy of the second French empire. Their activities were often controversially received at home, just as they were often romanticized later. But by example and through their writings they influenced and informed the whole of modern French colonial theory and practice. Bugeaud, however wrongly, was occasionally raised to the position of founding father of this unplanned dynasty. His efforts were favorably recognized, by Lyautey among others, as the first to deal effectively with a new sort of colonial situation which, however, would become the usual one in the empire of the Third Republic. Even as late as the 1950s, one of the last major colonial administrators and a historian at the Sorbonne, Hubert Deschamps, wrote unqualifiedly, "This school of French colonization, begun with the efforts of Bugeaud in Algeria, counted three masters: Faidherbe, Gallieni, Lyautey."

This may be stretching historical continuity beyond its tensile strength. However, more important is the realization that Gallieni and

Lyautey, as close associates and colonial soldiers exposed to a variety
of cultural experiences all within that ecological setting where population, climate, and terrain mandated that the French would have "possessions," not "colonies," were the two truly formative figures of the
new empire. Their successes, dramatic but not militarily exhausting,
gave colonial expansion an appeal it did not have before and showed
that a realistic approach to colonial policy, not one cast in abstract
thought, would allow the French to match the British in economy of
effort.

As the two most famous and respected upholders of that *ad hoc*
approach to colonial rule which was dubbed "association," they won
as important an ideological battle at home as any military battle in the
colonial world. The policy of association became the new dogma,
officially accepted between the two world wars. Its sanction was
recognized by Albert Sarraut in his *Mise en valeur des colonies françaises*.
In one of his introductory statements he offered the following: "The
French colonial operation, conceived for the well-being of both parties
. . . is an association—to use the felicitous formula which has become
the motto of our colonial policy."

However respectful the response to association had become, it
could not divert attention from the fact that colonial administration
was not regulated simply by theoretical considerations embroidered at
home or even policy decisions enforced in the field by outstanding
military administrators. The tension between direct and indirect rule
was a persistent fact of French colonial existence, and one that was
never satisfactorily resolved. Ultimately, colonial rule meant foreign
imposition: the realization of French goals, not indigenous ones.
Therefore, what was required from the local population was not really
cooperation, but acquiescence. No matter how nobly defined, the
colonial situation was not one of mutuality of partnership, but one of
subordination on the part of the people subdued.

Every advocate of the new "native policy" acknowledged this
condition and, furthermore, understood that the policy could work
only with the active participation of the governing elites and general
toleration—non-interference—by the majority of the population.
After all, colonial rule was alien rule and therefore was bound to be
culturally and socially disruptive.

If there was one region in which the French learned these simple
but unpleasant lessons, it was Indochina, which served in the second
half of the nineteenth century, much as Algeria had in the first, as the
military ground on which colonial administration was tested. But, in
stark contrast with the Algerian experience, Indochina witnessed a
series of French attempts to avoid direct rule, to link the French

conquerors and the local governments through the device of the "protectorate."

The existence of highly refined if unreformed governmental structures in the kingdoms comprising Indochina suggested to the French that control could most effectively be imposed through the state agencies already in place. Rule through the intermediary of local rulers and their representatives was the fundamental premise in the theory of the protectorate. Of course, the idea and the practice were neither new nor French. The Romans had tried the method in parts of their empire; medieval Europe was the scene of variations of it, both within and without the Holy Roman Empire; and even French officials of the 1860s considered British control in India to be to a large extent successfully based on this very principle.

The originality of the French effort, therefore, is to be found only in the fact that it marked a departure from previous French colonial theory and policy. Indochina was not to be Algeria, at least in administrative schemes. But once again harsh reality frustrated French thought.

No colonial beginning was less auspicious or carefully considered than that of the French in Indochina. Initially, they neither knew much about the peoples they set out to rule in the provinces in Cochinchina, nor had any clear purpose other than the military and naval one of securing forts and ports. Under the "regime of the admirals" an attempt was made at the protectorate form of organization. Admiral Louis-Adolphe Bonard, Governor of Cochinchina from 1861 to 1863, sought an administrative protectorate directed through the mandarin class, which, as in China, had long formed the bureaucracy of the land. However, the continuing military resistance of the population and most particularly the unwillingness of the mandarins to serve the French required direct French intervention and inhibited enlistment of indigenous support.

The situation in Annam eventually seemed more promising, although the Third Republic's colonial involvement there was marked by a decade of confused military and diplomatic activity. Not until the Ferry ministries of the 1880s did the French make a serious military advance against the Tonkin province, which bordered on China and was considered a political tributary of the Annamite empire. In that region the "Black Flags", by providing the Annamite government with military resistance to the French presence, caused the French considerable trouble. But Ferry's forward policy here also met with opposition at home. A treaty negotiated by Jules Harmand in Hué in 1883 was disapproved by the Chamber of Deputies which had not been consulted about it. Moreover, fighting with the Chinese, who intervened directly in Annam in 1883, was also cause for parliamentary alarm and recrimination.

Ferry managed to survive at home politically and to advance militarily and diplomatically in Annam. A new treaty was signed and approved in 1884. And in 1885 this treaty of protectorate over Annam was recognized by China. It is true that Ferry fell from power because of further French military involvement, but the emperor of Annam was also rendered powerless in the same year, 1885.

In Annam the protectorate idea was converted from a diplomatic to an administrative fact of colonial life. The first significant Resident-General in the new possession was Paul Bert, father-in-law of Joseph Chailley-Bert—an interesting fact demonstrating that the closely-knit "family" of colonial advocates had marital as well as ideological connections. Although Bert held his post for but one year, he instituted the practice of working through the Emperor and with the support of the local mandarinate. His illustrious successor, Jean de Lanessan, Governor-General from 1891 to 1894, intensified the new policy in Annam and also extended it northward to Tonkin, which Bert had left under direct military rule. In an influential study he wrote in 1889, *L'Indo-chine française*, Lanessan defined the policy he was to pursue and, simultaneously, offered as good a definition of the protectorate as can be found in French:

> Instead of attempting to order everything and do everything, let's leave the internal administration of the country in the hands of the Annamite bureaucrats, whom we will guide by our advice and whom we will surround with our control. Let's win over the intelligentsia and the people by the deference we show toward their institutions.

Although Lanessan no more achieved his objectives than his predecessors had theirs—or his successors would theirs—he demonstrated the value of the arrangement and did so coincidentally with the military activities of Gallieni and Lyautey in Tonkin. Of considerable importance in the development of this "family" of colonial ideologues was the influence Lanessan exerted on that new colonial officer Lyautey. In a letter to his sister dated November 16, 1894, Lyautey described Lanessan's approach as follows: "Establish a protectorate and not a system of direct administration. Instead of abolishing the existing elite, use it—govern with the mandarin and not against him.... There's the theory. I confess it fascinates me *a priori* because it proved *de visu* the absurdity of the other system, that of the bureaucrats in Algeria ...."

This early fascination with the protectorate would eventually travel with Lyautey to Morocco by way of Madagascar. But, before that journey was undertaken, the protectorate was implanted in North Africa, in the other of Algeria's territorial neighbors that the French claimed as their own. Between the military invasion of Tunisia in 1881 and the Treaty of Marsa of 1883, which established the diplomatic relationship between the two nations, the French pondered how they might resolve the dilemma immediately confronting them: expressed, in the phrase of the time, as "neither annexation nor abandonment." The solution, stipulated in the Treaty of Marsa, was the protectorate—an arrangement that not only mitigated opposition by interested European powers, by not being directly annexationist, but also seemed to produce good results quickly and on a large scale. The outward retention of the beylic government, the appointment of a Resident-General to direct French interests through the Bey, the attempt to utilize existing governmental agencies—these were all characteristics of the new system. The results seemed pleasantly astounding, such that Paul Cambon, the first long-term Resident-General in Tunisia, remarked, "Thanks to this system we were more the masters of the populations here in four years than in Algeria after fifty-five years of conquest." Paul Leroy-Beaulieu echoed these words in his 1908 edition of *De la colonisation*: "With this flexible, perfectible and humane regime, we were able to obtain in Tunisia, in a quarter of a century and without expense to metropolitan France, results that were more significant than those obtained in Algeria after sixty years and at a cost of considerable blood and 4,000 million francs."

Shortly after Leroy-Beaulieu's words were published, Lyautey, in Morocco, converted the protectorate into a governmental work of art. There he did everything within his means to preserve the semblance and reality of the Sultan's government. Even more, Lyautey, who once described the Cherifian Empire as a sinking boat, reconstructed this ship of state so that it would once again be seaworthy, as it still seems to be today. In effect, he established a diarchy—two vertical administrative lines of government services, French and Moroccan—meant to impose separation of function and thereby to maintain the integrity of the Makhzen, or traditional Moroccan political system.

With Lyautey's Moroccan work, the French colonial administration had acquired a definition nearly as far-reaching as the geographical proportions of the empire. Association and the protectorate, joined in theory and practice, formed the new alloy used to structure the empire from the Far East to North Africa. And the important quality of the alloy was its flexibility. As Gabriel Hanotaux, France's Foreign

Minister at the time, remarked in 1896, "The protectorate cannot be defined; it is a statement of fact and that's all."

Yet matters were not always so simple, as the situation in Indochina had already proved, and as the situation on Madagascar so blatantly demonstrated at the very time when Hanotaux provided his short definition. On that large island in the Indian Ocean, where they had been colonially involved since the late eighteenth century, the French now intensified their political action. After a series of hesitant diplomatic efforts at control, they finally, in 1895, imposed on the Merina monarchy a treaty of protectorate. Although the Merina were the major political power, they were but one of several island groups arranged in distinct and often competitive political units. With French acquiescence, however, the authority of the Merina had been extended to the point where it threatened to control the whole island, an arrangement the French initially deemed favorable to their own indirect, colonial control. However, mounting resistance by other island groups only led to further military complications, causing the French government to reconsider its policy.

This, in brief, is the background to Gallieni's arrival in 1896. Following the broad guidelines laid down by his government, Gallieni wisely implemented his *politique des races*, which, of course, implied variability of rule, not necessarily the protectorate system. He therefore established a method of domination that provided for treating the various ruling groups individually, and that served to contain the Merina. In some instances, as obviously with the Merina, the protectorate arrangement was maintained; with other groups, direct rule was imposed. By the time he departed, in 1905, Gallieni had demonstrated that versatility could mean stability: his political and administrative reforms were so successful that many of them remained in effect until after World War II and the era of decolonization. It is for this reason that critics almost universally acclaim the "colonial genius" of Gallieni, a man of action, of compassion, and of realistic outlook.

Yet it is interesting to note that, while Gallieni was exercising a variety of political options on Madagascar, Lyautey, who was happily serving under him, still believed that the protectorate form of governance should always win out. In his book *Dans le sud de Madagascar*, wherein he recounts his experiences, he argues that direct rule might briefly have been necessary in those regions on the island where military turbulence existed, but that on such occasions reestablishment of the traditional system should be encouraged once peace has been restored.

The protectorate thus continued to fascinate Lyautey, as it did most other imperialists of the era. Whatever its shortcomings, as demonstrated in Indochina and on Madagascar, it did seem remarkably adaptable and therefore eminently suited to French rule in those heavily-populated, traditionally-structured lands that comprised the major part of the new empire.

Modern practice, it might be argued, was designed for modern empire. In principle, the protectorate replaced administrative assimilation, and "association" replaced cultural assimilation. In thus attempting to break with their colonial past in administrative matters, the French of the late nineteenth century were facing the future, or so they thought.

As colonial rule turned out in reality, the French followed no set practice or form. Logic in a territory of 12.5 million square kilometers could maintain no symmetry. Thus, French rule had its pragmatic quality, conforming to local cultural and political configurations as much as to decrees run off in triplicate by some *fonctionnaire* in an ill-lit Parisian office. This said, one other important characteristic must be mentioned. As the empire became settled, pacified, occupied, and economically organized, the tendency toward direct rule increased. "Association" therefore never really worked so well as descriptive theory would have it. In all parts of the empire, even in Morocco after Lyautey's departure, bureaucratization implied more direct rule. According to the French sociologist Michel Crozier, in his *The Bureaucratic Phenomenon*, "these two opposite traits, the rigorous and constraining bureaucratic centralization of collective action and the spontaneous vitality of individualistic adventure ... remained until the end the two most permanent traits of the French colonial system."

The *beau geste* and the *règlement*—two national institutions that, placed side-by-side, make French colonial history a study in fascinating inconsistency.

Chapter Four

Empire in Fact

The era of the bush officer was giving way to that of the desk-chair administrator, remarked Maurice Delafosse in his *États d'âme d'un colonial*, published in 1909. Delafosse, a colonial official, was making reference to his own experience in West Africa. That he could so soon detect a change in the colonial situation is suggestive of the fact that the French Empire had passed from the stage of "paper" annexation, through that of annexation-in-fact, and had begun to enter the stage of general administration and development.

This process occurred before World War I and supports the argument that the major turning-point in French colonial history was not coincidental with the years 1914–18, but had appeared earlier, in the 1890s.

Yet there is no doubt that the World War proved to more than just the ardent imperialists that empire had its valuable national uses. To a beleaguered France the overseas possessions contributed a variety of raw materials, some of which—such as Moroccan phosphates, New Caledonian nickel, and Malagasy graphite—were of immediate importance to the military. Even more significant was the contribution in manpower: 519,000 soldiers from North Africa, Oceania, West Africa, and Indochina served a cause that was not theirs; and 184,000 workers from the same regions helped man the factories, till the soil, and service the ports, all left in need by national demands for French *poilus* to stand on the Western Front.

And, of course, there was that first class of graduates from the "school of energy" who sacrificed their lives for the France they so deeply loved. Ernest Psichari, frontier soldier and poet in Mauretania, died within the first weeks of the war. Joost Van Vollenhoven, Governor-General of French West Africa, quit that high African post in 1918 in protest over a government policy decision and returned to combat once again. He had earlier served in the war zone and escaped with a wound; this time battle claimed him. From Morocco most of Lyautey's old command also departed for combat, leaving behind a despairing Resident-General who suddenly felt beyond the grand sweep of history.

Even though the war imposed some dramatic moments on the French Empire, it exercised no immediate influence on the course of it. Essentially a European "civil war," the four-year holocaust left effects overseas that were neither so visible nor so scarring as they were on the old continent. Retrospectively, of course, the contemporary observer can see that the two world wars badly undermined all imperial structures and also fired a new spirit of national resistance. But in colonial, as opposed to global or "third world", history the war of 1914–18 provided few important dates.

In a very personal form, proof to sustain this assertion can be found in the autobiographical comments of Robert Delavignette, colonial administrator in Africa between the wars and later director of the École Coloniale, then retitled "The National School for Overseas France." In his little classic Service africain, he recounts how in 1919 he left his home in the war-torn region of Champagne and set out on a colonial career. What he then labelled the "France of Europe" seemed to him old, in contrast with the "France of Africa." He explained, "When I returned to the France of Europe, everything, even in those parts where attempts had been made to build anew and with a grand vision of things, seemed old and narrowly defined. In Africa, on the contrary, we were experimenting with the administration of the future . . ."

Delavignette's words complement in thought and spirit those voiced earlier by Lyautey. True, a new generation of colonial administrators had appeared, as the very person of Delavignette attests, but the best of these men saw their responsibilities and defined their aspirations much as had their colleagues who preceded them. In the eyes and minds of its agents, the French Empire still followed the general pattern marked out in the two decades before the war.

The key term associated with this phase of French colonial history is "development"—the mise en valeur of the various territories and their populations. Men such as Eugène Étienne and Joseph Chailley-Bert were asking in the 1890s how the empire could be made an economic benefit, and Albert Sarraut asked the same in the 1920s, as the title of his famous book suggests. Sarraut did even better than write: in 1921 he introduced into parliament a bill that he described as "a complete program for major public works, economic structures,

and social services." The description is a good summary statement of
what the French imperialists wanted done, even if it is not a résumé of
what they actually achieved.

To measure the economic and social effects of the colonial effort is
not an easy task. Not even a ledger of credits and debits, conceived
either in terms of capital invested and generated or in terms of trade
stimulated at home and abroad, can be prepared without intricate
qualification. Despite the copious statistics neatly arranged in government reports, the economic aspects of the imperial undertaking
were as haphazard, ill ordered and mixed in results as were any other.

Above all, there was high hope, inspired by a European "cargo
cult" of sorts, of heavily-laden vessels discharging their wealth
in the bustling ports of Bordeaux and Marseilles. The myth of the gold
secreted in the soil of West Africa, or the rich South China trade
waiting to be tapped through the river system of Indochina was briefly
matched in the 1950s by the dream of a "Eurafrican" community in
which France and Black Africa would join to generate GNP figures
impressive enough to allow favorable comparison with those of the
United States or the Soviet Union.

The realities of imperialism were much smaller-scaled. Morocco
and Indochina excepted, the empire never received the capital investment that its sponsors deemed necessary for economic success. But it
is even questionable whether such capital, under the conditions of the
time, would have done the trick. To recapitulate the argument of
Chailley-Bert, the possessions never did get far beyond the "age of
agriculture." Development, therefore, came to mean two particular
conditions: the intensification of existing agricultural activities and
trade patterns; and expanding the cultivation of crops and other raw
materials by the introduction of European institutions such as the
plantation and the concession company. Grain, sugar, rice, peanuts,
and ivory were among the most important of the materials that were
already being cultivated or traded; rubber, first in sub-Saharan Africa,
and then in Indochina, had become the principal new agricultural
product; and significant new mining interests had been developed—
notably the phosphates of Morocco and Tunisia, and the nickel of
New Caledonia.

Even the scope and order of the trade patterns seemed to be
characteristic of the era before capitalistic industrialization. First,
many of the transactions were of a decidedly seasonal nature. At the
time of the harvest, indigenous laborers would leave their traditional
pursuits and briefly enter the European economy in the capacity of
migrant workers, as in Algeria or West Africa. Or, if not so employed,
they would appear with the products of their land at harvest-time, to

trade these, either at European trading posts or through itinerant local middlemen, for the wares that the European merchants had to offer. The commercial houses on the west coast of Africa, for instance, were more like provincial shops displaying small quantities of household goods than like branches of modern companies. Cotton goods, hardware, and simple utensils were generally exchanged for peanuts or palm oil. It was all unimposing, far removed in tempo and scale from Les Halles or the Bourse in Paris, and bearing no relationship to Roubaix or Lyons. The new French port and commercial center of West Africa, Dakar, stood as a late nineteenth century monument to regional economic inactivity. A local French administrator who bore the improbable but appropriate name of Canard wrote in 1876, "Dakar is quiet, too quiet. Trade is practically nil, neither enough boats in the harbor nor people in the city."

Eventually, trade was stimulated there, as it was elsewhere, at the turn of the century, with modifications in commercial organization. The most notable change was the decline of the individual merchant or small company, now replaced by larger companies supported by more capital and enjoying far more extensive geographical coverage. But increased capitalization did not mean alteration in economic products. Throughout the colonial period, the agricultural base remained quite constant. If there was one dramatic change, it occurred in Indochina, in the French-created rubber industry, which began, following British success with rubber in Malaya, just before the World War. However, in the 1920s, the automobile industry, a postwar development throughout the Western world, gave new financial bounce to rubber production in Southeast Asia. Then, for the first time, large quantities of French capital were poured into the cultivation of this product, and the large-scale, corporation-owned plantations, such as those of the Michelin Tire Company, came into existence. It is important to note that, prior to the war, the Indochinese rubber industry was funded chiefly by locally generated capital, not by investments from metropolitan France—one further fact jeopardizing the "surfeited-capitalist" thesis of imperialism.

In the French possessions of tropical Africa and Madagascar, the commercial pattern was toward amalgamation and quasi-monopoly. Large companies in West Africa, such as the Société Commerciale de l'Ouest Africain, founded in 1907, grew out of combinations of smaller, family-run businesses, or new consortia of French entrepreneurs and bankers. Though the so-called Bordeaux *grands*—the largest and most prosperous of the family concerns—held on, they were pushed aside by the new concerns, which quickly expanded their range of business across the colonial territories, principally by means of small branches intended to cater to the restricted inland markets. Large concession companies marked the economic scene on Madagascar and in Equatorial Africa, where they controlled vast quantities of land. Yet this commercial experience was not one of great financial success; and, as much of the land was left unimproved, it was even less satisfactory in terms of agricultural development.

However, at their inception the concession companies of Equatorial Africa rose on a small "bubble" of speculation that resembled—but in geographically displaced form—the Louisiana "bubble" of the previous century. The apparent success of King Leopold II with concession companies in the Congo Free State—a success measured only in terms of the extra wealth it gained for the enterprising monarch—inspired the French. Speculation and excitement ran through Parisian financial circles in 1899, when, after argument and delay in parliament, the concession system received governmental sanction. Forty concessions were originally granted, covering some 650,000 square kilometers of territory, a veritable kingdom of private enterprise. The concession companies had domination of the land and its products, and were enjoined to meet governmentally established quotas, which would then entitle them to outright ownership of the land. In return, the government exacted a maximum of 15 per cent of their annual monetary returns in taxes. The effect, if not prescribed by law, was government by company, another colonial practice of the *ancien régime*. On commercial paper the scheme looked good, but in practice the view was dismal. The recruitment of labor, as will be discussed below, was difficult for the companies and appalling for the local populations. Transportation was primitive; and, with the introduction of rubber cultivation to Indochina, there was a decrease in the production and value of the principal marketable item. Some of the concession companies suffered deficit and collapse, yet the basic system, somewhat modified, was retained through the interwar period.

Whatever its organizational form, commerce remained the economic foundation of the French colonial empire. Capitalization, such as required in industrializing societies, was inconsequential. The hard fact is that only about 15 per cent of all French foreign investment went to the empire in the period immediately before the World War. The capitalization that did occur was local and circular: money generated in the colonial territory by Frenchmen resident there, and funds provided by the colonial government from taxes raised among the indigenous populations. Only after World War II was there a considerable influx of private capital and government financial aid from metropolitan France. The grand scheme of Sarraut and others for the *mise en valeur* of the empire depended on some government financial commitment. None of any note was made. The erratic money market in Europe after 1918 and the economic depression after 1931 warned the government away from this role. Moreover, growing political divergences in the approach to colonial problems, as manifested by the different views propounded by the Communists, Socialists, and traditional republicans at the time of the Popular Front government in 1936, had a debilitating effect. The new government's suggested plan, enunciated by the Minister of Colonies, Marius Moutet, was "a big program of small projects"—something of an inversion of the Sarraut *mise en valeur* idea, and designed to be of more immediate benefit to the colonized peoples. But this idea, too, failed to receive the parliamentary support it required.

And so, much like many other colonial interest groups, the Chamber of Commerce at Dakar had to be content to list one brewery, two manufacturers of lemonade syrup, and a freezing plant as the principal new business enterprises to have been established there during the 1920s.

Granted that these amenities made colonial life somewhat more enjoyable, and assured the displaced Frenchman that the local café would afford a refreshing pause in the day's activities, they give no particular proof that colonial society was truly "modernizing"—or that its white members had that competitive urge which Karl Marx thought led the European bourgeoisie to create wonders overshadowing the pyramids.

Few who lived in it ever claimed that the colonial world was a place of limitless opportunity. Some Frenchmen did become remarkable entrepreneurs, it is true, and thereby did turn a handsome profit—although the historian will have to look closely to find an individual in French controlled territory who did nearly as well as Cecil Rhodes, Thomas Lipton, or, later, J. Harry Oppenheimer. In addition, there were selected members of the indigenous population who found capitalism to be a wonderful, because an enriching, foreign intrusion. At the other end of the scale of comfort, however, were those *petits blancs* who received a poor salary and eked out a dull existence, living in sullen disappointment in a land they did not know and despised. Their African and Asian counterparts were deeper in despair, performing tasks of grueling labor in order to make Sarraut's *mise en valeur*, of which they knew nothing, something of a reality. Somewhere in the middle of this socio-economic scale were the small farmers, settled principally in Algeria and the old colonies of Martinique and Guadeloupe, but also in Indochina and Madagascar. Most of these real colonists lived modestly, removed from both the culture into which they had intruded and the culture that the French colonial administration had imported.

The very range of interest and purpose among the various individuals placed in the colonial situation was itself a factor militating against concerted success. Over and over again, the *colons*, merchants, and entrepreneurs were in opposition to government policy. The merchants in Tonkin province, for instance, complained bitterly about the introduction of French justice in 1896, because its comparative leniency—the abolition of corporal punishment, for example—complicated the task of retaining workers, who were now less impelled than before to respect French contracts. In Equatorial Africa, French concession-company personnel were distressed in 1906 when the government forbade the establishment of "native reserves" as originally planned in the concessions, and thus prevented the displacement of the population from lands the companies coveted. And, in Morocco, Lyautey engendered both governmental and private resentment by his efforts to restrict the zone of French colonization.

Inversely, the role played by local administrators was often one of acquiescence to the demands of the merchants or *colons* and, therefore, of disadvantage to the indigenous populations. The worst effects of this policy occurred in Equatorial Africa, where concession-holders used brutal methods of rounding up labor, including the taking of hostages and the burning of villages. For this activity the government, to ensure that the requisite numbers of laborers were obtained, supplied troops.

Finally, in this conflict-ridden colonial system the French, in their capacity of administrators, often added a distorted dimension. Aside from the outstanding military administrators, of whom Gallieni and Lyautey head the list, the quality of the French in the colonial service often left much to be desired. Not until the École Coloniale was founded, in 1889, did the French government attempt to discriminate in its selection and to take care in the training of its administrators. "Before 1914," wrote Hubert Deschamps, "colonial careers had a bad reputation in French opinion. It was generally agreed that only second-raters were sent there. This was a myth . . . ." Not quite. Historical study has shown that, if not always second-raters, the men who serviced the French Empire were often ill trained, often ill disposed to the people they ruled, and, generally, uninspired.

Of the many occupations that might attract an able member of the upwardly-mobile middle classes, service in the tropics was not high on the list. This can be readily appreciated. Living conditions were generally adverse, with climate and disease taking their toll of the Europeans on duty. For the ambitious, the empire was no "school of energy," but a place of lethargy where the supervision of some small community or the clerkship to a colonial governor was accepted only as overheated boredom. Talent, as is well known, is socially formed, turning toward those professions that are in demand, honored, and well remunerated. None of these conditions prevailed in the French tropics.

That French officers in Algeria and Tunisia pulled down magnificent Roman ruins in order to build forts suggests that not all of those serving in the colonial world were endowed with the cultural vision of a Lyautey. In West Africa the low quality of personnel was frequently mentioned in late nineteenth century official communications, with successive governors lamenting that only those incapable of succeeding at home ventured abroad. And nearly everywhere there appeared regular reports of incompetence and misjudgment, these interspersed with occasional reports of cruelty in the administration of the local populations.

The most infamous case of cruelty by administrators was the Gaud–Toqué affair. Gaud and Toqué, minor officials in Equatorial Africa, were tried in 1905 for crimes they were accused of commiting in 1903, when they sought Africans for the system of labor and porterage that the concession companies required. The list of their cruelties was extensive, running from starvation to the execution of a prisoner by discharging a stick of dynamite attached to his body. This particular killing, Gaud had said, "will petrify the natives. After this, they'll not raise a murmur."

On the contrary, more than a murmur was raised, and in official French circles. A full-scale investigation was undertaken, although the government refused publication of the results. Both Gaud and Toqué were sentenced to five years of solitary imprisonment, but their sentences were soon reduced to two years. What the French public did learn in the process was the cruel treatment of the population by colonial officers clearly unworthy of the positions assigned them.

Certainly the record of French colonial personnel in action was not totally blemished. The point is, it never was as distinguished as the imperialists had anticipated it would be, in those early days when empire was noble, not routine. Delavignette, who saw so much well—and from the perspective of irony, which is the only angle from which to see the grandiose and pretentious—described thus the relationship of the administrator to his post in Africa: "a discreet marriage in which one is too tired to be unfaithful."

For better and for worse, the French and Africans and Asians did hold together, if seldom working in a spirit of genuine cooperation. The key to empire growth was labor—on this point all theorists agreed. But the French were informed by a bourgeois ethos that equated work with morality: civilization was defined, in this context, as regularity of labor. Although the colonial world was in the age of agriculture, too many French administrators approached it as if it were an integral part of capitalist industrialism. The type of laborer they had in mind was timed by the factory whistle and motivated by the paycheck. Delavignette commented in the 1940s that in Africa the French administrator treated his subjects as if they were "hands," when in reality they were peasants.

The cultural differences accounting for the patterns of work that the French found among their subject peoples were unappreciated and led to severe, subjective judgments that were contemptuous in tone, often racist in implication. One of the least offensive appears in a letter written in 1878 by the Senegalese administrator Louis Canard. He commented, "The natives are forever exhibiting an unusual laziness, and it is very difficult to get them to work. Outside of the lugger service, which scarcely occupies them four months a year, they do absolutely nothing but dance and beat their awful tom-toms." In Equatorial Africa, the Gaud–Toqué affair was preceded by many complaints that the Africans were economically worthless and, according to a few critics, should therefore be exterminated.

French labor policy was founded on deep-set misunderstanding and severe divergence of purposes. Moreover, as it was developed into practice, this policy was resented for its severity by the indigenous populations. What the French soon resorted to was far removed from the concepts of a "free labor" market preached at home.

As with all of the other colonial nations, France tolerated the principle of forced labor. In the initial phases of colonization, the common social mechanism was the *corvée*, an institution that had burdened the French peasantry under the Bourbon monarchy. But the *corvée* was not a French or even a European innovation. Its equivalents had long existed in, for instance, Indochina and Madagascar, with the French thus continuing an old practice there. What the *corvée* consisted of was compulsory labor, of a set number of days, on the construction and repair of public-works projects, notably roads and railroads.

Colonial officials considered the *corvée* the quickest and most effective device by which to construct the "infrastructure" without which the market system could not function. Even as humane an administrator as Gallieni introduced the colonial *corvée* into Madagascar soon after his arrival, with two decrees of October 1896 and January 1897 stipulating fifty days of such labor per year for every healthy male between the ages of sixteen and sixty. In Cochinchina in 1897, the term was set at thirty days. Very soon, however, the *corvée* was abolished in most areas or, more accurately, transmuted into a poll or head tax (the *prestation*), which forced the population to seek employment in European projects or to raise cash crops, in order to find the means of payment. In fact, labor impressment continued in one form or the other to the end of World War II.

Two striking examples were provided in the interwar years, and, owing to their violation of the code that the International Labor Organization of the League of Nations had adopted concerning the employment of native labor in colonized countries, both cases aroused international indignation.

The first occurred on Madagascar and bore all the marks of military regimentation. In 1926 the governor created the Service de la Main d'Oeuvre pour les Travaux d'Intérêt Général, which mustered young Malagasy, by means of service camps and enlistment for periods of two, then three, years, into construction tasks, most particularly the building of the Fianarantosa–Manakara railroad. Although these individuals were paid a minimal wage and supposedly limited to a forty-eight hour week, their labor was grueling and exacted in a manner inconsistent with the humanitarian purposes the French had long advertised. How hollow now seemed Sarraut's statement made but three years earlier: "The French colonial operation is no longer the spoliation of one race by another."

Sarraut's words would next ring with the sound of brass when the full dimensions of the labor scandal in Equatorial Africa were revealed. In this territory the wanton waste of human lives, already appalling in the system of porterage employed in the 1890s, was intensified with the construction of the Congo–Ocean railroad. A project considered as early as 1886, construction of this railroad to link Brazzaville to the sea was not undertaken until 1922. Between that year of initiation and the year of completion, 1934, nearly 150,000 Africans were utilized in its construction. Of that number 120,000 were *recruités*, whose services were obtained by a system of impressment. In what was one of the most flagrant violations of International Labor Organization restrictions on forced labor, the colonial administration in Equatorial Africa, by a decision (*arrêt*) of 1925, established a system of quotas for the number of laborers to be taken from each province. "Recruitment" of this force produced the most abominable of results in the practice of forced labor: tremendous attrition in lives, starvation, uprooting of families, destruction of villages where recalcitrance was encountered. And, in addition, there was that peculiar form of modern cruelty: mass-produced annihilation. "I have need of 10,000 dead for my railroad," commented Governor-General Raphaël-Valentin-Mauris Antonetti.

Part of this dismal story was told academically at the time by the American Raymond Leslie Buell, in his pace-setting study *The Native Problem in Africa*, published in 1928. Another perspective, both more dramatic and more personal, was provided by André Gide in his *Voyage au Congo* (originally a series of articles he wrote, beginning in November 1926, for the *Nouvelle Revue Française*), which provoked public indignation, but, lamentably, not an official investigation. Not until 1946 was forced labor abolished throughout the French colonial territories.

The social relationship that labor policy such as this established between colonizer and colonized was generally strained, based on the contempt or indifference of the one, and the suspicion and fear aroused in the other. Once again, it is Delavignette who knew it so well. In his novel *Les Paysans noirs*, first published in 1931, he starkly describes the colonial situation as follows: "Thus the country was divided in two: the miserable peasants who worked for the White and hated him; and the clever chiefs who profited from the White while scorning him."

Labor policy was not alone in generating tension and difficulties between colonizer and colonized. One other aspect of the *mise en valeur* which proved troublesome socially was education. That this should have been may initially seem surprising, given that no social benefit was considered more important in French imperialist ideology than the "elevation of the minds" of the subject peoples. Even after assimilation had been cast aside, the *mission civilisatrice* persisted, as befitted a people proud of its intellectual attainments.

Education in the empire was beset by problems of implementation and conflicting, or ill-defined, goals. The lack of trained teachers, the shortage of suitable text-books, and the limited funds available were obstacles to any plan that might have approached universal education for the colonial public. Moreover, French intentions often encountered indigenous resistance. Among the Arab populations, as among the Annamites, the French educational system was an alien force, undermining traditional religious education and the values it inculcated. And, among other peoples whose agrarian way of life was satisfactorily fixed, the need for the written word did not have the quality of a categorical imperative; folk wisdom stood well against the publications of the Maison Hachette.

The growth of French education, in scope and in acceptance, was directly correlated to the administrative institutionalization of French rule. At the beginning, in the era of exploration and conquest, French needs for educated personnel were rather limited and primitive; generally, only an interpreter who knew sufficient French to act as go-between or negotiator was required. However, the establishment of a colonial bureaucracy, the appearance of more merchants and plantation-owners, and, finally, the arrival of a sufficient number of French families to require the opening of French-type schools altered educational needs and patterns everywhere.

This new colonial overlay imposed a different set of social values on succeeding generations. Education was now seen as the means to betterment, to admission into the "French club", even if only as a very junior and easily dismissed member. In Camara Laye's autobiographical novel of African life, *The Dark Child*, published in 1954, the young hero undergoes, as he grows up, this new and foreign *rite de passage*, by working his way through several levels of colonial education. Before he leaves his home for technical school in Conakry, Guinea, his father enjoins him, "Make the most of your opportunity. And make me proud of you. I ask no more." The thought was colonial French, not native African, and expressive of the values now placed on advanced study within the French-designed educational system.

Significantly, French education preceded French colonization in many parts of the empire. The Catholic missionary effort was an extensive and an old one, as the work of Père Marquette in Canada and Albert de Rhodes in Annam attest. On Madagascar, to cite a major instance, Anglican and French Catholic missionaries engaged in an imperialism of minds and numbers that was more intense than any of the "missionary imperialism" of the early nineteenth century in Oceania. Indeed, the high level of education in Madagascar after the imposition of colonial rule was in part owing to the continuing effort of these French missionary groups. Even after the system of *écoles officielles* was introduced by Gallieni in 1899, private education retained an important position. Following an initial precipitous decline, in the years immediately following the 1899 decision, the number educated at private schools rose again, so that in 1931 it stood at about 66,000, or rather than more than half the corresponding figure for the public system (111,000). In Algeria during the early days of colonial rule, the White Fathers, an order founded in the 1860s by the priest–imperialist Charles Lavigerie, did important, if limited work. Toward the end of the century, the Holy Ghost Fathers were introducing religious education—as were the American Protestant groups—into the Congo and Gabon at the time when the French were imposing colonial rule there. Yet, before either of these activities, in the Senegal of the 1850s, Governor Bouet-Willaumez utilized two French-trained Senegalese priests to establish a secondary school in St Louis. This was a doubly important innovation. One of these priests, the Abbé Boilat, was perhaps the first African enthusiast of French culture to attempt to spread the gospel of his enthusiasm among black African students.

Historically, however, he is more important as the author of the *Esquisses sénégalaises*, the first analytical survey of Senegalese culture by an African—and an unusual example of the continuing missionary interest in local cultures.

Throughout the history of French colonial empire, therefore, the missionary effort in the field of education was a major one. However, with the installation of the Third Republic in France, the parochial educational issue became a political one, because anticlericalism was made an important domestic issue in the 1880s. Thereafter, the role of religious schools in the colonies was countered by the development of a secular school system. Yet, even with this new expansion and competition, the number of subject peoples educated under colonial rule remained exceedingly small, with the exception of Madagascar. Indeed, Madagascar seemed to be an incredible exception, with, in 1931, 32 per cent of the island's school-age population actually enrolled. In striking contrast, Senegal, in 1938, had something less than 1 per cent of its school-age population enrolled—a sad fact in view of the tradition of educational expansion begun by Faidherbe in the 1850s. Even more unusual seem the statistics from Algeria, the oldest and most assimilated of the units of the new empire. There, in 1944, only 1.6 per cent of the total Arab population was receiving some sort of European education. In simple fact, public education was a very restricted matter, in purpose as well as in numbers.

If there was one common characteristic of educational policy in all quarters of the empire, it was the calculated avoidance of the introduction of the domestic French system as a global solution to indigenous needs. A popular base for this attitude existed, one that extended far beyond the colonial situation. Pedagogical theory in the era of early imperialism was suffused with the same social Darwinian thought that helped shape the colonial policy of "association." Intellectual variations were then considered to be both conditioned and fixed by heredity and environment. Thus, the "subtle" French mind was accepted as a product crafted by centuries of cultural evolution and, therefore, impossible of re-creation in an alien environment. The peculiar divergences of intellectual make-up that environment was thought to determine led to a widespread acceptance of educational relativism. In colonial considerations a sort of "nativist" attitude emerged, in which the intellectual possibilities of the subject peoples were either discounted contemptuously or appreciated comparatively. Whichever position was assumed by administrators was of no consequence to the general conclusion that no Sorbonnes should be built abroad.

There were, moreover, more immediate concerns that shaped

educational policy. What the French required in their empire was not philosopher-kings but semi-skilled workers and low-level bureaucrats. As the Gallieni administration in Madagascar put it, in an ordinance dated April 16, 1899, the objective was "to make the young Malagasy faithful and obedient servants of France, to provide an education which, in form, would be industrial, agricultural, and commercial so as to ensure that the settlers and the various public services of the colony can meet their requirements in personnel." Some twenty years later, Sarraut, then Minister of Colonies, said much the same thing in a circular he sent to the various colonial governors. Education must essentially be "practical and realistic in character," he stated.

Between the two dates in which these statements appeared there were some notable attempts to systematize education. Although no one can deny that educational flexibility was more a characteristic of the French effort than was rigidity, the institutional pattern was pretty much the same throughout the colonial territories. As early as the 1870s, the French were constructing a three-tier system in Indochina, with schools at the local and provincial level, plus a few advanced primary schools or *collèges*, located primarily in Saigon. The basis of selection for advancement was, in principle, demonstrated talent, but higher-level study was meant to attract children of the traditional elite, the mandarinate, and thus involve them in the new French system of things. The language of instruction at the lowest school level was the vernacular, as it was in Madagascar following Gallieni's decree of 1899 instituting a three-tier system there. French served as the language of instruction only at the more advanced levels. However, under the three-tier system created in 1903 by Governor-General Ernest Roume in the newly founded Federation of French West Africa, French was the language of instruction at all levels; and in 1925 the same system was introduced into French Equatorial Africa.

Despite a great deal of carefully considered organization, education in the colonies remained limited in quality and extent. For most of the minority of young people who were trained in the French system, education ended at the village school, where they were taught to read, write and do simple arithmetic. Throughout the empire, the principal institution of higher learning was the teacher-training school, or *école normale*,—which should not be confused, as regards curriculum or instruction, with its French equivalents. Of all the upper primary schools established in the colonial period, perhaps none was more famous than the École William Ponty, founded in 1903 and located in Dakar. Offering work in pharmacy and the law in addition to training for primary-school teachers, this school educated an impressive number of the future leaders of independent Africa, who continued to feel a sense of fellowship, as "old boys", long after they had graduated.

Education outside the colonial context, particularly in France, was not precluded, however. Between 1866 and the late 1870s the colonial administration in Indochina sent a number of young men from Cochinchina to study in France. The experiment was not deemed a success and was therefore allowed to fade out. Then, in 1885, Félix Faure, Under-Secretary of State for Colonies, founded in Paris the École Cambodgienne, an institution designed to arouse in the children of Indochinese notables an appreciation of French culture, so that relations between colonizer and colonized would improve. In 1889 Eugène Étienne, in the post that Faure had held, caused the school to undergo a considerable change. Retitled the École Coloniale, it still trained a very small contingent from Indochina, but was thenceforth primarily concerned with the training of French administrators.

Between the world wars the French university opened its doors to a handful of exceptional youth from overseas. Although a university had been established in Algiers in 1879, and another—although scarcely meriting the name—had been founded in Hanoi in 1903, young people from all over the French colonial world made their way to Paris, where the "native" student soon ceased to seem an exotic item. Occasionally, such a student even assumed a significant position in French society. Between the wars Léopold Sédar Senghor, future President of Senegal, who had studied at the École Normale Supérieure, taught at the prestigious Lycée Louis-le-Grand in Paris. In the same period Félix Eboué, a black from French Guiana who had studied at a *lycée* in Bordeaux and then at the École Coloniale, occupied first the governorship of Guadeloupe and then that of Chad.

The key to success was, of course, knowledge of the French language, which eventually made its way as *lingua franca* throughout the colonial educational system. The French themselves often expressed doubts about using only their own language, but their reluctance to learn the local language, their high regard for their own culture, and their realization that a more elaborate administration required greater participation by the local people combined to assure the ascendancy of French. Frantz Fanon, a colonial subject from Martinique and now posthumously famous as a "third world" philosopher, indicated the importance of the language issue in his classic, *The Wretched of the Earth*. Writing of a growing self-consciousness and revolt against colonial ways, he commented, "Suddenly the language of the ruling power is felt to burn your lips." French meant the taste of French culture. French colonial administrators accepted this point, often ardently upholding it.

The most interesting problem arising from selection of the language of instruction appeared in Cochinchina and lasted through the second half of the nineteenth century. There, modernity and ideology encountered tradition and philosophy. The debate centered around *quoc-ngu* (meaning "national language"), an early missionary creation designed to romanize the writing of the Annamite language, which effort administrators and missionaries intensified after the French occupation. *Quoc-ngu*, it was hoped, would avoid, even eventually eliminate, the use, in Annamite, of Chinese characters, which were a carrier of Chinese thought, notably Confucianism. The missionaries had found the romanized approach most satisfactory for evangelical purposes, but some colonial administrators saw it as a means of diminishing the impact of traditional thought on local politics, of warding off the heavy influence of Chinese civilization, and of introducing a new cultural idiom of real value as propaganda. The lack of written materials in *quoc-ngu* remained a major problem and in part explains its slow progress northward, beyond Cochinchina. Nonetheless, the French decided in 1878 that *quoc-ngu* and French should be the only official languages in Cochinchina.

By the end of the century *quoc-ngu* had won the battle of the books, but French, too, was enjoying a victory. At first *quoc-ngu* was the language employed at the early primary level of instruction, with French restricted to advanced primary schooling. Later, however, a striking change was introduced by Albert Sarraut, who in his educational reforms of 1917 required French to be the language of instruction at all levels and in all schools. This clear "assimilationist" move by one of the staunchest advocates of "association" did not go unnoticed and was supported by some but attacked by others of the Vietnamese intelligentsia. Subsequently, one of Sarraut's successors reverted to the old compromise. Throughout the interwar period, the educational issue had the quality of an ideological one, which intensified as Vietnamese nationalism, a highly literary movement, grew more bothersome to colonial officials.

French concern with the revolutionary potentials of education was expressed early. Many officials acknowledged that the training of the mind in a new mode of thought and with a new set of purposes would be disturbing. In one of the most famous résumés of the organization and purpose of colonial education, a circular submitted to colonial officers in French Equatorial Africa in 1925, Governor-General Antonetti remarked,

> In this agrarian land it is a very serious matter to uproot a
> child from his natural vocation for the soil. Those who
> undertake to do so must assume full responsibility. . . .
> what remains important is that no one leave school without
> first having the means of suitably acquiring the necessities
> of life and of maintaining a family.

The first worry, then, was with possible frustration of "rising expectations." No matter how poorly or narrowly educated, the young
people who entered the French school system formed part of a new
elite, one often rebellious against its culture-of-birth and anxious
about its culture-by-forced-adoption. In the interwar period, student
movements emerged that demanded reform such that the gallicized
youth could play a more important role in the colonial system and
enjoy more fully its advertised benefits. Government reaction to most
of these movements was unsympathetic, often repressive. Certainly
the famous Larousse Dictionary motto, "Je sème à tous vents," was
not one the colonial administration cared to adopt.

Both labor conditions and educational development would figure
prominently in the rise of reform and resistance movements, as would
the impact of returning servicemen from both of the world wars.
However, as colonial unrest, frequently registered throughout the
interwar period, grew to new proportions, it appeared to be disturbing to some French observers. Interestingly, Sarraut acknowledged
this potential problem in the preface to his *Mise en valeur des colonies
françaises*, where he considered "the re-awakening of aspirations
which might not be without danger for European civilization the day
when they brought together the old fanaticisms, nationalisms, and
mysticisms against the enlightenment coming from the West." Yet
he, like so many others, assumed that French rule would endure into
the foreseeable future, with soon-to-be realized promises standing as
assurances to, not burdens upon, the subject peoples.

Indeed, it was in the interwar period that the terms "empire" and
"France Overseas" entered the popular vocabulary, thus indicating
that the overseas possessions had been structured in the French mind
somewhat as they were in reality. If there was one proof that suggested
to the popular mind the solidarity of the empire it was the performance
of the Force Noire, the black African troops who had served so
gallantly on the Western Front. After the war a series of personal
accounts were published, each attesting to the courage, loyalty and
good spirit of these troops. In the preface to his study of 1934, *La Vérité
sur les Tirailleurs sénégalais*, Édouard de Martonne summed it up thus:
"The black army is today not only an element in the *colonial army* but

also an integral part of the *national army* and for that reason merits being known and appreciated at its true value."

Plans for the extensive use of black troops had been drawn up and debated in the last decade of the nineteenth century, but it was not until 1912 that a recruitment policy, and funds for it, were voted by the French parliament. Yet ever since the creation of the Tirailleurs Sénégalais by Faidherbe, such troops had been used in colonial wars. Gallieni had employed them in Madagascar in 1896; they served in Algeria in 1909; and they would be used in Morocco to quell the famous Rif Rebellion in the late 1920s. However, Lieutenant-Colonel Georges Mangin popularized the issue of their use in a series of articles, published collectively as *Force noire* in 1910. Mangin envisaged black African troops as the means to compensate for the declining French birthrate, hence the declining number of young men available for military service. With the two Moroccan crises, which staggered European diplomacy at the time, the French manpower shortage caused worry and, consequently, acquiescence in the plan sponsored by Mangin.

Although the original intention was to use black African troops in the colonies in order to allow French soldiers stationed there to serve in Europe in a time of national emergency, units of the Force Noire served in large numbers in France during the World War. Moreover, under a government plan of 1918 that made Blaise Diagne, a black African deputy from Senegal, High Commissioner for Recruitment in Africa, provision was made for their systematic recruitment. This continued after the war, with about 10,000 young Africans drafted annually to serve France. The recruitment often amounted to impressment, as many French authorities were willing to acknowledge; but the action was justified as a "blood price." In the words of A. Messimy, a French parliamentarian writing on the matter in 1909, "Africa has cost us enormous amounts of gold, thousands of soldiers, and seas of blood. We don't expect to get the gold back. But the men and blood must be returned by Africa to us with heavy interest." Severe on the African, the policy was encouraging to the population in France and, moreover, regarded as a testimony to the purpose and success of empire. One book published in the interwar period was entitled *Peau noir, coeur blanc*—"Black Skin, White Heart"—a combination that epigrammatically expressed a French ideal, if nothing else.

Although these may be seen most clearly on the colonial maps that were printed after the war, the major lines of development marked thereon were prepared in the prewar era.

The government at home and the governors abroad had assumed, before national attention was riveted on the war front, that their principal task was consolidation. With this in mind a number of federations were formed: Indochina in 1879, West Africa in 1895, and Equatorial Africa in 1910. These federal systems, ruled by governors-general, advised by federal councils, and enjoying substantial budgets, were favorably reviewed, in the postwar era, for their administrative and economic efficiency—although in both domains they actually had mixed results.

Certainly on organizational charts and wall maps the systems held together. Their rail networks had grown enormously and were heralded as the means to economic development and extended international trade. In Indochina alone, some 2,000 kilometers of track had been laid down between 1898 and 1910, including the very costly Transindochinois, which connected Saigon with Hanoi. In French West Africa in 1904, during the Governor-Generalship of Ernest Roume, the Sudan railroad was completed, and, between 1900 and 1903, rail construction in Guinea, Dahomey, and the Ivory Coast was undertaken. Although some major rail construction took place after the war—principally in Madagascar and Equatorial Africa, and at a cost in human oppression that has already been discussed—the major lines were planned and in large measure constructed before the war.

As one imperial network took form on land, so did another appear on the oceans of the world. Although not so grand or so famous as the British "red line of empire," the French system was impressive nonetheless. And it was old-established as well. A service from France to Argentina by way of Dakar, Senegal, had been established in the 1850s by the Compagnie des Messageries Maritimes, founded in 1851 under a slightly different name. With a government contract signed in 1881, the company extended its eastern service to Australia and New Caledonia, by way of the Suez Canal. It thus serviced a vast territory, and in this was soon accompanied by another major maritime concern. The Compagnie Maritime des Chargeurs Réunis was founded in 1872 chiefly for service to Latin America, but it soon heavily concentrated on port trade along the west coast of Africa. In 1899 the company obtained the license for the official French mail service on that coast, and at about the same time it increased its number of banana boats, so giving the newly-established banana plantations increased incentive. In 1902 the company began direct service to Indochina. Yet other companies plowed the waters of the Mediterranean or hugged the coast of West Africa, so that, all in all, a colonial traveller before 1914 could progress somewhat comfortably and without undue delay around most of the littoral of the empire.

No one will doubt that the regular development of such maritime services provides interesting statistics to ponder retrospectively, just as such services attracted trade and must, therefore, be considered in any imperial reckoning. Nevertheless, by the early twentieth century romance no longer went down to the sea in ships. Thereafter it journeyed with two new forms of transportation, neither of which was of major commercial value at the time, but both of which were eminently newsworthy.

In the interwar period the automobile not only rolled along the cobblestones of Parisian boulevards, but also bounced over ill-defined routes in Africa and Asia. Automobile clubs appeared as newly-imported French institutions. And with them came another characteristic of modernization, the *rallye*. On the occasion of the centenary of the French occupation of Algiers, in 1930, the automobile clubs of Algeria and Tunisia organized a trans-saharan rally that went from Algiers to Gao and tempted forty-six automobiles, all of which succeeded in completing the trip.

Yet this particular automobile rally was of primary interest only because it was organized around standard, production-model automobiles, and with infinite care about supplies, lodging, radio communication—and newspaper publicity. Years before Commander Jolly was accompanied by Madame Blasselle in Car Number 1, other teams were traversing Africa by motor. Through the imagination and money of André Citröen, often called the "Henry Ford of France," the "Citröen Caterpillar Tractor Expedition" had been organized to cross the Sahara. Departing from Tuggurti in southern Algeria in December 1922, the expedition arrived in Timbuctu in January 1923, having traversed the 2,000 miles in twenty days.

Citröen was soon anxious to repeat his success more boldly. In 1925 he arranged the "Citröen Central African Expedition," an undertaking that would have pleased, but not surprised, his fellow countryman Jules Verne. The expedition travelled from Algeria to Mozambique and then, by ship, to Madagascar. Its purpose was to test the feasibility of road transportation and, also, at government request, to trace a route for a projected trans-African railroad, still a dream in the official imperialist mind. Eight ten-horsepower Citröen automobiles equipped with rear caterpillar treads made their way across the African terrain, and with anticipated adventure. In the Sahara desert, the leaders exercised nocturnal caution, fearing "robber bands." The cars were arranged in a square, and mounted machine-guns were prepared for the worst. "But our improvised fortresses were never attacked and the only sounds that broke the oppressive stillness of the night were the steady tramps of our sentry and the occasional yelp of a lonely jackal." So commented the expedition leader, Georges-Marie Haardt.

However, this hint of the romantic quality of overland travel should not be allowed to hide the rather impressive effort the French were making with road-building, particularly in North Africa and Indochina. As early as 1909, the American publication *National Geographic* ran an article entitled, "In Civilized French Africa," wherein its American author expressed great praise for the French as latter-day Romans who construed empire as an engineering problem in road-building. "They are building for the future," he brightly commented, "they are planning a hundred years ahead in everything they do; they are using these great roads as a means of opening up the country just as the railroads have opened up our great West."

While he exaggerated the promise he saw along the roadway, his praise was not far amiss. During the interwar period, Morocco and Indochina were both endowed with impressive road systems, if not with many automobiles to travel over them. Even in West Africa there was some commercial transportation by motor truck, which was seen as the most feasible means by which to move goods over short distances in a region where the river system was ill defined and allowed only for seasonal transport. The early arrival of motor vehicles in the region is highlighted by a Dakar Chamber of Commerce report of 1910: this states that there were one bus and one car in the city—and complains that poor roads inhibited the importation of more.

Despite increased road-building, automobile travel remained difficult, occasionally hazardous, between the wars. Provisions and services were still in short supply, while the ever-present problem of unwanted sand produced obvious effects. And so a lengthy automobile trip was often classified as an expedition.

What the gasoline engine did to the rough terrain of empire, it would also do aloft—but with even more drama. Before the World War some Frenchmen had visions of large airships cruising the sultry air of Africa and maintaining the *pax colonia* at a safe altitude. Nothing came of these early schemes, and what promise they may have had plummeted to earth with the former Zeppelin *Dixmude* (then the property of the French navy), which crashed in 1923 while on a training cruise of Africa and the Mediterranean.

Heavier-than-air craft provided a different story. After 1909, when Blériot proved that water could be negotiated by a propellor churning the air, the conquest of international space followed the conquest of foreign land. In the French sphere, one can find no more impressive example of the intrepid aeronautical spirit than that of Pierre Latécoère, a pioneer airplane constructor and founder of the Ligne Latécoère, which established service between Toulouse and Barcelona as early as December 1918. Yet Latécoère's intentions were more extended. Even in 1918 he hoped to link Europe to South America by air. Being a Frenchman, moreover, he approached the problem at right angles, an aerial system going from Toulouse to Dakar, and then from Dakar to Buenos Aires. On May 12, 1930, the first flight across the South Atlantic was successfully made.

Latécoère mustered an able group of pilots, one of whom gained great fame as a writer. Antoine de Saint-Exupéry joined the Latécoère company in 1925, the first year in which the Casablanca–Dakar run was executed. The trip was an intricate game of aerial hopscotch, with planes making ten stops between the two points, and carrying an Arab interpreter in case of a forced landing.

Saint-Exupéry's major writings concern his experience as a pilot in Africa. Although not an imperialist, he had the appearance of a new centurion, the guard who defended the aerial boundaries of empire. Certainly he relished life in this African world, with its invitation to individual action, just as Lyautey or Delavignette or—the best comparison—Ernest Psichari had done. Psichari the poet and Saint-Exupéry the novelist found the Sahara an immense space that could be contained within the heart. *Le Petit prince*, Saint-Exupéry's classic, is not far-removed in tone from the highest colonial aspiration. And *Terre des Hommes*, much more attractive in its English title, *Wind, Sand and Stars*, is autobiographical adventure, a story told around the colonial empire, if not of it.

In this remarkable work, Saint-Exupéry provides the reader with a marvelous little tableau concerning a little colonial scene.

> From my very first trip I have known the taste of the desert. We were stranded ... near the fort of Nouatchott. This little post in Mauretania was then as isolated from all life as an island lost in the sea. An old sergeant was stationed there with fifteen Senegalese. He received us like messengers from heaven.... He cried. "In six months you are the first. Every six months they supply me."

Empire meant many things and appeared in many images, as Saint-Exupéry unintentionally states here.

Empire in fact was frequently harsh for the African or Annamite laborer to endure; it was, perhaps, an inspiration for the *diplômé* of the École William Ponty; and it was a vocation, a calling, for the young Delavignette and the old Lyautey. It was the location of solitude and beauty for Psichari and Saint-Exupéry. Finally, in 1940, when the Third Republic collapsed before the thrust of the armored divisions of a new empire, Hitler's Third Reich, *France d'outre-mer* took on a special and poignant meaning.

With the government in disarray in the port city of Bordeaux, to which it had fled, a number of high officials, including the President of the Republic, decided to set sail for North Africa, where they would set up a government-in-exile. Their plans were thwarted, but that such plans could have been considered at the time suggests that the empire stood firm in fact and hope to Frenchmen who otherwise could only despair of the future.

The French generally continued to observe strict European protocol in the Colonies. In this probably idealized drawing, French officials observe protocol at Fashoda.

n early French commercial establishment in Saigon, 1864.

A print of about 1835 showing the seizure of Mascara (Image d'Epinal).

Marshal Bugeaud's stately presence at the Battle of Isly in 1844.

TROOPS IN ACTION

A patrol of the French Chasseurs d'Afrique, 1881.

A march-past of French Colonial Troops at the Centenary of Algeria.

Some members of the 43rd Battalion of Tirailleurs Sénégalais.

General de Gaulle on his visit to Brazzaville in 1958.

The Americans in Morocco during the Second World War.

Two buildings in Dakar. *Above* the Colonial Governor General's palace. *Below* a modern maternity hospital in the "Niger style".

Chapter Five

Empire in Form

The Sears-Roebuck Company of Chicago contributed an easily
assembled model of Mount Vernon, George Washington's home, to
the Parisian International Colonial Exhibition of 1931. Such a trans-
position of architectural style and residential tastes was not always so
easily done or so well received in the colonial world, but that it was
done is obvious. The durable forms of French imperial intent still stare
haughtily at the visitor, even if their occupants, functions, and proper
names have changed. Urban development, the most noticeable topo-
graphical change in nineteenth century Europe, eventually became a
major characteristic of colonial empire also.

Indeed, the colonial city has been considered by many contemporary scholars to be the nodal point at which European and indigenous
cultures converged, from which the colonial influence was extended
to the countryside, and out of which later emerged the new elites who
sponsored the movements for national liberation. Therefore,
although few French colonial cities attained a size or acquired the
amenities of a French provincial city, they were outsized in their
historical significance. And, today, they are the doubtful legacy left
behind to countries they were unintended to serve.

Of course, the city was not a colonial innovation. Timbuctu, for
instance, seized the French imagination for a good century before the
French acquired the Sudan in which it is located, and it stood as a
center of Moslem commerce and learning for some five centuries
before then. Hué in Annam, Kaiouran in Tunisia, and Fez in Morocco
were major urban places long before Louis XIV turned his attention to
beautifying Paris. Nor, when they put together their second overseas
empire, were the French themselves newcomers to urban development in a colonial setting. New Orleans, Montreal, and Mobile are

among the several impressive examples of previous French city construction—and each is as much a monument to sound urban planning and good taste as it is to colonization.

The new colonial cities that the French built served quite different purposes from these, and it is therefore in function that the city of the modern imperialist era differs from its predecessors. In Africa and Asia the village, town, and city were often spatial representations of a particular cosmological system or else major religious centers. Angkor Thom in Cambodia was the "City of Gods" and still gives testimony to its sacred purposes in its magnificent stone carvings. Kaiouran, constructed in the ninth century, was and remains a major Moslem center, famous for its mosque. The early colonial cities also had particular purposes: they were French settlements, constructed to serve the needs of French colonists particularly.

The new imperial cities appeared to be foreign extrusions from the soil on which they were placed. Either administrative or commercial centers—and frequently both—they housed an itinerant population of Europeans, a displaced and seasonal population of Asians or Africans, and they faced outward as parts of an imperial system that seldom served the hinterland. Yet they were primate cities—the center of colonial life in all of its manifestations, and the focal point toward which the indigenous populations moved in hope of new opportunities.

The attractive qualities—socially magnetic and aesthetically pleasing—of the new colonial city nevertheless appeared rather late, not until the twentieth century, and most noticeably between the two world wars. Prior to this time, the major metropolitan centers developed by the French overseas were few, and mainly confined to the Algerian littoral. The French communities there (the largest and almost the only sizable ones in the overseas empire) had come into existence as a result of privately-sponsored colonization, the transportation of political exiles during the reign of Napoleon III, and the resettlement of refugees from the lost provinces of Alsace and Lorraine after 1870. Even after just the first two decades of French colonial rule, the coastal cities of Algiers, Bône, Oran, and Constantine had European populations in the thousands. Among these, then and later, the most important urban center was Algiers.

Algiers was anything but a French creation, of course. Its location had been scouted and utilized by the Phoenicians, and after their time the city became a major Moorish capital and a pirateer's haven. It was an urban center of major proportions before the French entered it in 1830. Subsequent to this action, the city changed character: a French urban grid was superimposed on it, and future growth was European, not Arab, in purpose and form. Primarily intended to be a military base for the newly-installed French army, Algiers was soon the major supply center for the colony.

The military effects on this city's structure cannot be exaggerated. To construct its barracks and parade-grounds, the French army destroyed some of the major monuments and structures in the Arab quarters, thus spatially intruding into and violating the center of the old city and its famous casbah. Later, expansion was outward, but in the initial phases the process was one of demolition and reconstruction, resulting not only in social tensions but also in the wildest forms of real-estate speculation and poor residential construction, as French profiteers suddenly saw a bourgeois form of El Dorado glittering before them. In 1839 some 15,000 Europeans inhabited Algiers; in 1847 the number was nearly 43,000. The numerical growth explains what happened.

Amidst the rubble and the rabble that this demographic change generated, colonial Algiers took form. By the middle of the century four newspapers greeted those who could read French; a theatre, constructed by municipal funds, played four times a week to a house of 500—if all the seats were sold; and a variety of cafés catered to the different layers of emerging *algeroise* society. A development plan had been considered by the government as early as 1846, but its implementation was delayed, save for one major feature. This, a work that since its completion has received universal praise and has stood as the new city's particular architectural signature, is the Boulevard Front de Mer, which faces the sea and was constructed on a rhythmic series of arches, behind which were located warehouses for the port. Begun in 1860, with the first portion opened in 1866, the whole provides a magnificent façade before the old city and stands as an example of stylistic tastefulness in a colonial period of municipal destructiveness. A visitor in 1860, Ernest Feydeau, offered the following description in his *Alger*: "Alas, when looked at close by, Algiers today seems more designed to dull the eye than to brighten it. A lot has been spoiled, made ugly, or destroyed. And the sad part of it is that the Europeans alone are guilty of these acts of vandalism."

Such a comment was never registered about the second imperial city of the nineteenth century French Empire—a city that, as late as 1905, had a total population of just 54,545, of which only 8,749 were French. Saigon was known as the "Paris of the Orient", a sailor's delight and a Frenchman's pride long before the city was transmogrified into an American commercial strip in the 1960s. Before the French occupation, it had been the provincial capital of Lower Cochinchina. Bordered on the east by the Saigon River, and with the village of Cholon neighboring it on the west, it was soon marked out, by the French, to serve imperial purposes, and eventually became the chief port of the Indochinese Federation, with the export trade in Mekong Delta rice providing it with a bustling maritime commerce. It also became the seat of the Lieutenant-Governorship, and thus the capital, of French Cochinchina.

The eleventh edition of the *Encyclopaedia Britannica*, that impeccable compendium of scholarship and style, thus advertised Saigon to its wide readership in 1911: "Double rows of trees give shade in all the streets, the width and uniformity of which, together with the beautiful gardens, make Saigon one of the finest towns of the Far East." A more refreshing, if acid, commentary on the city's urban condition comes from an insider who first arrived in Saigon in 1894. This was the ubiquitous traveller and voluminous letter-writer Hubert Lyautey.

After having viewed Singapore, which impressed him with its spritely commercial activity and generally attractive appearance, Lyautey was already predisposed to disappointment. His first impression of Saigon was summed up in the comment "lots of sham." What he found was a pretentious administrative capital, not a lively commercial city, with everything official approaching the monumental. "The general aspect of all this cardboard decoration situated in this magnificent vegetation is very satisfying, pleasing to the eye," he remarked in a letter dated November 10, 1894. The following evening, arriving for dinner with Governor-General Lanessan and his wife, Lyautey could not resist commentary on the magnificence of the new governmental palace.

Yet what Lyautey saw just before his carriage stopped under the portico was an example of the new imperial style. At that time the French colonial empire was entering its own short-lived Augustan period of serenity and anticipated magnificence. The new Ministry of Colonies occupied the prominent Pavillon de Flore in the Louvre, and thus was projected onto the center of Parisian life and into one of its most elegant edifices. A few years later, in 1898, Dakar would be considered by the government a major naval station, to be outfitted to serve French interests throughout the South Atlantic. And, as noted in Chapter 2, a rich literature on empire was making its appearance in bookshops, while the imagined exotic qualities of the overseas world were richly presented in paintings, poster art, and mantelpiece baubles. On many levels form preceded function, or anticipated it, as an oversized appreciation of what the imperial dream might become was publicly displayed.

Perhaps it was Gallieni's admonition, *bâtir en dur*, that suggested the urban and architectural purpose that the French started to follow at the end of the century. New structures were designed to suggest new administrative functions and to impress upon the indigenous populations the permanency and power of the French occupation. Again, Lyautey is the authoritative narrator, this time speaking of Gallieni's town-building in Lang Son (in north Vietnam): "In the middle is the future residence of the Colonel, almost a palace, but so conceived to affirm French power . . . ."

Among the best examples of this empire-of-grand-scale is the construction undertaken in Dakar. Shortly after this sleepy little town of , in 1884, 9,084 inhabitants had become the capital of the new Federation of French West Africa, Governor-General Roume, whose term of office began in 1902, was planning on a grand urban scale. New roadways were laid out and new barracks planned, and a central post office and town hall were projected. When, in 1914, the design of the post office was made the subject of a competition, the guidelines as to what was required stated, "The planned building will be one of the most important monuments in Dakar. It will be visible from all points in the harbor and the lower city. . . . . It is therefore desirable from an architectural point of view that the building provide an imposing and original exterior aspect."

When eventually finished, the post office did not compete with the palace of the Governor-General either in the grandeur of its façade or in the amount and strength of denunciatory criticism that it attracted. This ponderous structure, begun during the Roume administration, rose on the highest bluff in the city, one facing the sea and dominating the land. The wrought-iron gates, cast in France and designed to define the entrance to the forecourt, were considered imposing enough to be made part of the French exhibition at the 1904 St Louis Exposition. And so they stood first in the United States before beginning their seaborne journey to the new federal capital.

Even before the tricolor was ceremoniously hoisted above its cupola, the palace was the subject of derisive criticism. It continued to be so until it was modernized in the 1950s, with cupola, portico and a few other trimmings removed, a renovation indicating changing imperial times. A special correspondent for the *Écho de Paris* stood before the structure in 1929, and described it as follows to his readers:

> This much must be said for the palace in which Monsieur Carde [then Governor-General] resides: it is ugly. It is of a massive ugliness, obsessive, definitive. It suggests what can happen in the brain of an architect, who is not evil but delirious, when he combines the pseudo-style of Palladio

and Louis XVI. What stands here is monstrous, pretentious, and insipid.

Certainly this was not the result intended by the imperial mind, or by
the architect who followed its wishes. Both were attempting to define
the beginning of a new colonial era, one of peace, wide-ranging
administration, and general prosperity. Whatever its architectural
shortcomings, the palace of the Governor-General marked a new
phase in sub-saharan colonial urbanization. Like Indochina and North
Africa, this colonial region also was being submitted to the structural
forms of modern European civilization.

Throughout most of the nineteenth century the colonial city grew
slowly. In fact, "town" or "village" is usually a better description.
With the exception of the few places settled by Europeans—such as the
old-established towns of Point-à-Pitre on Guadeloupe and St Louis on
Réunion, or the towns on the Algerian coast—the colonial centers
seemed impermanent, very rudimentary in social condition. Most of
them bore a resemblance to American western towns of the same era,
with, perhaps, the café substituting for the saloon. It was the haste of
construction, the extensive layout of the land, that invited comparison, and this did not escape the attention of the ever-observant
Lyautey. Of Gallieni's efforts in Lang Son he stated, with unmitigated
enthusiasm, "Sensations of America: a town is born on empty
ground. The streets are laid out on a grand scale, the first construction
is but four months old . . . and some fifty houses are already partially
built, according to a rectangular American plan." In his novel *Le Chef
des porte-plumes*, the French colonial novelist Robert Randau complained at, did not praise, what he saw as Dakar's sudden, American-
like rise early in the twentieth century.

Whether positive or negative, such comparisons suggest the fascination that the United States as a continental empire held for the
French mind, and they also suggest certain distortions. What Lyautey
commended Gallieni for was exhibited elsewhere and was not originally American. The grid urban frame was characteristic of most
French colonial cities. It marked eighteenth century St Louis in
Senegal, and would form the basis of the first plan for Dakar, drawn
up in 1856 by Jean-Marie Pinet-Laprade. The virtues of such an
arrangement were in engineering: the construction of streets and the
installation of basic sanitary features, such as water pipes and sewer
lines. Throughout the colonial empire there existed what might be
called a "water line", defining the possible extent of urban development. Such a "water line" was heavily drawn in all of Africa, where
there was not only an obvious and critical need for drinking water, but

where such a supply was required for vegetable gardens, for wetting down the unpaved streets in the dry season, and for watering the trees and shrubs that the French used to shade and embellish the major thoroughfares. In 1902, according to the Chief Engineer of Bridges and Roadways, Dakar was capable of supplying only 300 cubic meters of water daily, this coming from four pumps found close to the sea. Inhabitants living on the plateau area had their water rolled in barrels.

To speak of urban planning in the colonial territories prior to the twentieth century is to discuss water supply, road-paving, and sewerage. These problems remained to plague colonial engineers until the end of French rule. Moreover, that such fundamental matters of sanitation were unresolved does in part explain the problems of disease that harassed Europeans and indigenous populations alike. On the island of Gorée and then in the city of Dakar, each decade seemed to be accompanied by its particular yellow-fever epidemic. In 1816 the survivors of the shipwreck of the *Medusa* endured another calamity when yellow fever ravaged their camp. Not until the outburst of 1878 did the authorities construct a hospital in Dakar.

Bubonic plague worked its way up the coast in the first decade of the twentieth century, arriving in major force in Dakar in 1914, and causing sanitary and political problems of the most serious order. A large number of the Lebou tribe, the dominant ethnic group in Dakar at the time, lost their lives from the disease, and general African dissatisfaction with the colonial administration's handling of the epidemic led to a civil disturbance in November 1914, so serious in its proportions that the Lieutenant-Governor of Senegal requested that the Governor-General declare a state of military siege. This was averted, but a decision to relocate the African population in a separate area, so that sanitary control could be guaranteed, was read as an act of flagrant segregation. The creation of the "Medina" in Dakar became a political issue, one already of sufficient importance to play a role in the election of 1914, which resulted in Blaise Diagne becoming, as deputy for Senegal, the first black African in the French parliament.

Social patterns, too, followed a rough pattern of development. In most of the colonial cities in their initial stage, the chief European representatives were young men working for commercial establishments and hoping to gain sufficient revenue to return soon to France, which itself was frequently called "the most beautiful of French colonies" by them. As late as May 1923, the Chamber of Commerce at Dakar stated to the Governor-General that "to make a good employee and above all an employee with a future and a perfect colonizer, the candidate must come to the colony at a young age. . . .

the age which is best for the satisfaction of these exigencies and characteristics is seventeen on the average."

The fact that the cities housed a young, celibate population greatly conditioned the structure of life. The popular building form in most urban centers consisted of two stories, the upper of which served as a dormitory, fronted by a verandah to protect against the sun; and the lower of which served as the shop or warehouse in which the merchandise for the local trade was sold. Little residential discrimination existed, and, as can be anticipated, the taking of mistresses led to a mulatto social element in most cities in Africa.

The second professional grouping, often the most important numerically, was the military. Thus the barracks and dormitory-warehouse were the most characteristic nineteenth century colonial structures. Nevertheless, compliments to the military for its efforts to house troops on colonial service were few. Lyautey expressed the greatest disfavor with the military situation in Saigon. The small size of, and number of beds in, the dormitory rooms created what he considered intolerably cramped conditions. In addition, he complained about the insufficient washroom facilities and the lack of recreational facilities. The most serious of his charges concerned the location of the barracks, their long axis on a north–south line, meaning that sunlight streamed in all day. Nor were there blinds to provide interior shade. A health mission to Senegal in 1901 registered similar complaints, stating that the lack of sufficient verandahs on the barracks there made for grave discomfort.

Then and later, French critics argued that architectural plans were imported from metropolitan France without any consideration having been given to local conditions and what they entailed in human needs. However, the impermanence of the population in the colonial city and its peculiar social make-up were strong factors in determining the unattractiveness and rudimentary nature of living conditions. Only in the interwar period did noticeable changes in social structure bring commensurate changes in cultural life. True, well before then, Algiers and Saigon had good municipal theatres, several newspapers, and fine boulevards with a variety of shops. Elsewhere the urban atmosphere was provincial at best, dull not dazzling. By an ordinance of 1879, the municipality of Dakar forbade the beating of tom-toms after 10 p.m., and in 1907 the Chamber of Commerce of that city requested the government to outlaw the blowing of ship whistles after sunset.

Two major changes altered this sort of urban scene: the first occurred within the colonial environment, the second was a European problem. First, the successful campaign waged against tropical diseases, which, as killers of Europeans, led both Indochina and West

Africa to be labelled "white man's graveyards," greatly reduced risk in the colonial environment. The efforts of branches of the Institut Pasteur, against malaria in Indochina and yellow fever in West Africa, led to important research and subsequent control of these diseases. Drinking water was better filtered and available in greater supply, while tinned foods greatly supplemented products found in the local environment. As a result, soldiers and merchants were more willing to bring their families with them, the younger more willing to take their brides on a "tour" of colonial service.

Secondly, the economic depression that hit France in the 1930s made the colonial world more attractive as the possible location of satisfactory employment. Families now ran the risk of seeking their livelihood in the colonies. Moreover, with the weakening of the metropolitan economy, the bi-annual vacation in France became an expense that was often too burdensome to be borne. There was, therefore, less circulation between homeland and colony; hence, a greater fixity of the European population.

Largely as a result of these new conditions, the Eurafrican and Eurasian city took on a more domestic appearance. French schools proliferated, pastry shops appeared, and so did hairdressers and clothiers. Breweries were an additional mark of the flow of civilization, as were movie houses. Now suburbs added to the urban measurement, these providing the setting for the villas in which the wealthier Europeans lived, their homes now illuminated by electricity. Rail services increased, and in some cities, such as Algiers and Casablanca, tram and bus services allowed for a daily demographic displacement comparable in form, if not in scope, to that usual in the European city. The automobile was no longer a curiosity, and the bicycle gained first place as the most popular form of transportation. Most obvious and socially most significant was the emergence of a new tertiary sector in the economy, as gardeners, maids, washerwomen, and child-nurses were sought among the indigenous population by French families. The word "boy," an obvious English importation, which took its place in the new colonial vocabulary at the end of the nineteenth century, became a widely-applied term.

Accompanying these social and cultural changes were the first true examples of urban planning. Although the colonial government of Algeria had prepared a plan for the development of Algiers in 1846, little came of this. And in 1856 the first plan for Dakar was drawn up by Lieutenant Pinet-Laprade, as mentioned earlier. However urban-conscious they were, and however influential their Cartesian perception of the real world, the French were somewhat slow in introducing legislation regulating urban planning. Of course, Baron Haussman

had renovated Paris during the reign of Napoleon III, for which effort
he has been acclaimed and damned ever since. But the first general
French law on urbanism was passed on March 14, 1919, by which all
cities with populations of 10,000 and over were required to have a
"plan for lay-out, beautification, and extension." Of some interest,
the first French conference on colonial urbanization was held in conjunction with the Parisian International Colonial Exposition of 1931.

What ought to arrest the attention of the modern observer, however, is the rather remarkable progress made in planning and style
before 1919, at a time when urban agglomerations were still primitive
in shape and social purpose. The coastal regions of Africa offered the
most scope for urban action. In part this was owing to the smaller
number of major cities already existing there, and in part it was the
result of a pre-colonial economic network that made internal trade
more important than coastal trade. The most significant French urban
development, because imperial in purpose, took place on the coast,
where small fishing communities, such as the one on the Cape Verde
peninsula, gave way to imperial cities—what Dakar finally became in
name and style in the interwar period.

An architectonic imperialism appeared early, but was more evident in plans for monuments and public buildings than in actuality.
However, several fantasies, eclectic blends of pagoda roofs or Moorish arches with European Romanesque, for instance, appeared at the
international expositions from 1889 on. In the colonial world, however, the most pronounced effort was toward the exportation of
European styles, or melanges of them—as in the instance of the
Governor-General's palace in Dakar.

What may be described as the first serious effort at stylistic consis-
tency or harmony began in Algiers, particularly during the
Governor-Generalship of Charles Jonnart, whose tenure all but spanned the first decade of the twentieth century. Then, the French
administration took an admiring look at the indigenous Moorish
styles and decided to draw on them in designing new public buildings.
The resulting *style Jonnart*, as it was called, adorned the prefecture
building and the main post office, both characterized by ceramic
mosaics, Moorish arches and ropelike columns. The style was criticized soon enough by colonial officials—of whom Lyautey was the
most prominent—and by Algerians themselves, both groups deeming
the results mere ostentation and parody.

The most serious, successful, and praised effort to strike an
architectural and urban harmony between French colonial intentions
and indigenous values was made by Hubert Lyautey in what became
the French imperial showcase: Morocco. But what he achieved in

Morocco was the realization of plans and ambitions that had grown throughout his colonial career. His admiration for English colonial urbanism, his appreciation of Gallieni's efforts at Lang Son, and his own experience in the construction of a town at Ankazobe, Madagascar, in 1897–8 preconditioned his activities in Morocco.

As an ardent urbanist, he was the first to articulate in thought and practice the "two-town" concept of development in French African cities. Just as the policy of association meant the juxtaposition but distinction of the two cultural groups involved in the colonial situation, so colonial urbanism implied, he argued, the need for the same relationship. "On the one hand, out of respect for the native and in our artistic and aesthetic appreciation of these ancient cities and monuments; and, on the other hand, out of respect for our profound respect for their family and religious traditions," the French would create new cities, not destroy the old ones, he announced.

The impact of Lyautey's ideas, like the effects of the urban plans drawn up by his chief agent, Henri Prost, were noticeable throughout Morocco. Furthermore, Lyautey's aesthetic approach marked a new departure in architectural thought among French colonial administrators. Rejecting heavy "romantic" pastiche styles, such as had been used in Algeria, he insisted that authentic Arab art was without ostentation and characterized by a simplicity of line and façade. More significantly, he assumed that the revitalization of indigenous art had to come from within, not from without, and this through the encouragement of local artists in the traditions of their own culture.

The urban activities that Lyautey directed in Casablanca made it the premier city of French colonial urbanization and admired throughout the French colonial world. A revitalized Moorish style defined the new Medina constructed in the city center, while the linear simplicity and subtle Moorish motif of the new government quarter suggested a distinctive approach to colonial architecture. That the new palace of the Sultan was the first major building constructed, this in 1916, gives some indication of the official relationship Lyautey wished to maintain between art and politics.

In sub-Saharan Africa a similar search for a harmonious "native" idiom that would serve the colonial purpose was undertaken after the World War. The Neo-Moorish influence filtered down from North Africa, but it was overwhelmed by a "Neo-Sudanese" or "Niger" style developed from the style that had captured the imagination of the French when first they reached Djenné and then "Timbuctu the mysterious". In the 1920s and 1930s, a modern version of this style, distinguished by its Sudanized pylons, its imitation of red African earthen materials, and its use of crenellation, was easily realized in reinforced concrete. In Dakar it defined the new maternity hospital and the new market-place; in Bamako it appeared in the large, central market; and in Bobo-Diouloasso it appeared in the railroad station.

However, this affectation of a "colonial" architecture was matched by a new interest in an "imperial" one. Just as the term "empire" gained in popular resonance between the wars, so the desire for something grander in urban layout worked its way into administrative thought and action. Nowhere was this sentiment given more obvious physical expression than in Dakar.

In function Dakar had acquired a veritable imperial status. Granted administrative autonomy in 1924 and expanding to fill its role as the center of an economically growing West African federation, the city was transformed. What one critic called the "haussmanization" of Dakar—the growing tendency toward the construction of the monumental building and geometrically regular roadway—was already under way. The central square, the Place Protet, was faced in 1930 with a new Chamber of Commerce building, one of the largest buildings then constructed, but in the Ionic style of the Louis XVI era. Equally unsuitable to the local setting was the new Roman Catholic cathedral, begun in 1923 and inaugurated in 1929. Its architects produced a pastiche of Byzantine and Neo-Sudanese styles, heavy in appearance and solemnly dedicated to the memory of France's early colonizers.

Bold measures to give order to the rapidly growing city were proposed in the urban plans submitted in 1931 by the government-appointed urbanist M. Toussaint. Among his proposals were the construction of *rond-points* to control automobile traffic; distinction of the European and African sectors by laying out parks between them, punctuated by statues representing the two cultures; and, grandest of all, the recasting of the Place Protet, suitably enlarged, as the "Place de France," the pivotal point of the far-flung West African empire. In the center of the square would stand an elaborate statue representing "France bringing abundance to her colonies." Defining the inner limits of the square would be well-formed façades, fronted by graceful arches for the comfort of pedestrians. Finally, each of the avenues entering the square would be provided with a monumental gate, decorated in allegorical subjects. That Toussaint indicated a personal respect for the *style Niger* suggests how confused colonial intentions and imperial style had become almost everywhere outside the Morocco of Lyautey.

These plans were not realized, but they seem modest and dull in comparison with another set of plans, also unrealized. What Algiers might have become if reorganized according to one of the many plans submitted for it by Le Corbusier one can only conjecture. But, from the moment when a committee entitled "Les Amis d'Alger" invited him to the city, in 1931, this Swiss-born French citizen, one of the most influential architects of the modern era, took a deep interest in the project of Algiers' renovation.

Le Corbusier began with the assumption that "Algiers has ceased to be a city of colonization; it has become the central point of Africa." Convinced of Algier's "magnificient future," proclaiming that "the hour of urbanism has struck in Algiers," Le Corbusier unleashed his imagination and conceived grandly. As Caesar did Gaul, he divided the city into three parts: a *cité d'affaires*, or monolithic trade mart; a European residential section; and a civic center. The subject of the Arab quarter aroused warm passion: "The adorable casbah, which might be renewed, . . . must never, no never be destroyed!" he commented.

Between 1930 and 1942 Le Corbusier drew up three major plans: bold, awesome, frightingly technocratic; and causing the mayor of Algiers to say in wonder: "But these are for the next century." The piercing monolith that eventually was realized as the Ministry of Education building in Rio de Janeiro first appeared in sketch here; so did the ribbon-like structure that finally was curved into the UNESCO building in Paris. Also making a two-dimensional appearance in these rather utopian plans was a road of reinforced concrete that would have provided an ingenious solution, or so Le Corbusier thought, to the two desiderata of modern urbanism: good means of vehicular circulation; and sufficient public housing (apartments were to be constructed as part of the roadway's support).

While certainly not an imperialist like Lyautey in his proposed colonial undertaking, Le Corbusier nonetheless saw from the perspective of empire. The first sketch for his *cité* indicated that the building would have a north–south axis, not for the sake of lighting conditions, but as a symbol of relationships between Europe and Africa. His monumental series of plans, drawn up in 1942, were accompanied by two freehand maps of Africa, one showing an axis running from Paris to Gao in West Africa by way of Algiers, and with the inscription, "The great European–French–African current, will it pass through Algiers?" The other showed two arrows, one labelled "European," the other "Moslem," with the accompanying inscription: "Algiers, point of contact between occidental and indigenous civilizations." It is not too much to infer that, while Le Corbusier certainly did not see the future of Algiers as that of a "city of colonization," he did see it as that of an imperial city, a grand monument of European technocratic power—imposing in the direction of the sea, dominating in the direction of the hinterland.

Le Corbusier's original plan called for the creation, on the farthest tip of land, of a *cité d'affaires*, to be connected with a *cité de residence* by a concrete bridgeway. His final plan, that of 1942, suggested the division of the city into two distinct residential areas: the Arab, centering on the casbah, with its particular focal point, the old mosque; and the European, off to the east of this complex, with its center the *cité d'affaires*. Between the two, an elaborate civic center would serve as the cultural link, as the scene for the meeting of the two cultures.

Whether intentionally or not, Le Corbusier's plans fitted well with the changes in colonial policy and social development that characterized interwar Africa. Moreover, they pointed up a major problem in architectural form and colonial design. The two lectures that Le Corbusier was invited to deliver to "Les Amis d'Alger" were concerned with modern architectural techniques and their role in urban development. Technological change, most evident in the use of reinforced concrete—which was a French-invented construction material—appeared at a time when the social composition of the colonial city was almost everywhere changing. The influx of new categories of Europeans and the growth of new economic functions for the indigenous populations suggested that there was now a problem of urban mass and cultural fission.

The relationship between the two major social groupings had been largely decided by the "two-town" architectural–urban scheme proposed by Lyautey, Toussaint, and Le Corbusier. Although not so intentioned, all of these plans implied a cultural, even a racial, segregation. Such an arrangement was not new in the French colonial empire. As early as the 1840s, General La Morcière had removed the Arabs of Oran into the Djali, or "foreign" quarter. The "Medina" in Dakar, as has been suggested, resulted from a decision concerning hygiene, but was racially segregationist nonetheless. And Cholon, the village next to Saigon, grew rapidly as a local "native quarter," resulting in an increasing *de facto* residential segregation there. There is no doubt, however, that Lyautey's plan was based on cultural respect. As he put it in a speech delivered in Paris on November 10, 1926, "The European building with its many stories, or the modern skyscraper increasing in height, means the death of the landscape, a mortal blow to traditional life. Customs and tastes are in opposition."

Much the same criticism can be levelled against this urban arrangement as is frequently registered against the British concept of "indirect rule." Both attempted to "hold the ring," to isolate so as to allow development along traditional, non-European lines. But the

European presence was by its very nature a disturbing influence. New urban demands, of both an economic and a political sort, made the old way of life impossible to sustain. The wage-economy of the port, the externally-directed commerce, the European tax base, and the municipal government itself were alien to the indigenous urban culture and successfully competitive with it. Moreover, as the city grew, the "native quarters" became increasingly isolated. Overcrowded with people, undersupplied with public services, and ringed in by a European sector, they became blighted.

The particular problem of the "two-town" plan and of urbanism in general was further aggravated by the fact that able urban planners such as Lyautey and his remarkable assistant, Prost, were very few. Lyautey's departure from Morocco, followed quickly by Prost's, weakened the urban planning of Morocco, for their successors were individuals with less determination and sense of direction. The constant rotation of French colonial personnel often prevented an urban plan from being seen through. This condition had been complained of by Henri de Lamothe, Lieutenant-Governor of Senegal, in a letter dated December 6, 1891, to the Under-Secretary of State for Colonies. Discussing the problem of organizing and regulating building in Senegal, he lamented," despite all of the dedication and good will of each of the members [of the commission], it has been impossible, because of the excessively frequent rotation of personnel, to arrive at the objective desired. . . ." In addition there were conflicts of interest: between the military and the colonial administration, over land use; and between the municipal government and the colonial administration, over urban planning. Finally, there was no effective overall control asserted by Paris. According to Colonel E. Weithas, an engineer writing on the subject in 1932, "the cities in French West Africa have since the beginning of the conquest grown according to plans due especially to the initiative of local administrators, just as the houses have often been constructed according to the wild fantasy of private initiative."

After the Second World War the colonial urban scene was dramatically revised. Urbanism had become a subject of study for political scientists and sociologists who were concerned with the modernizing, as against the colonizing, process in the Third World. Technocrats replaced colonial administrators; planning was a carefully contrived socio-economic activity, "rationalized" in the Weberian sense of the word. For other reasons Hanoi, Saigon, Algiers, and Tananarive could no longer be called colonial cities; rather they had become metropolitan centers of political confrontation between new elites anxious to assert their authority against the older colonial administration and the social groupings that surrounded it. As for the seemingly-secure colonial territories in sub-saharan Africa, they witnessed new, rapid, and confusing development, as Dakar, Abidjan, Conakry and Brazzaville mushroomed. High-rise buildings sprang up and immigration grew, while elaborate *plans-directeur* intended to regulate regional as well as urban growth were laid out (as, initially, for Dakar in 1945). In all of this, urban development proved to be a catalyst of social change.

At no time was the colonial city a melting-pot, but it was soon a concourse for the diverse populations and interest groups comprising French colonial society. The physical juxtaposition of these groups and the close relationships of the functions they performed made not for a hyphenated community, as in the United States, but for a compounded one, easily described in the terms "Eurafrican" and "Eurasian." Outwardly, there were few signs of discrimination. There certainly was no "color bar," with services and facilities segregated. Increase in his economic and/or professional status usually implied, for the Asian or African, entrance into some, perhaps most, aspects of French society. But the superficial success of urban assimilation, as seen in St Louis or Dakar, Senegal, should not tempt the conclusion that the French colonial city was cosmopolitan in the way that Paris has so frequently been said to be.

If the colonial city had a particular characteristic, it was provincialism. The most obvious reason for this quality was the geosocial nature of the French minority who made up the colonial elite. Most of the French who settled in the colonies as merchants or administrators were of petty-bourgeois origin, members of provincial families themselves. Hubert Deschamps, the distinguished colonial administrator and historian, stated in a historical reminiscence of the African colonial situation between the wars that "the majority [of administrative recruits] came from the provincial petty bourgeoisie, that very numerous middle class, often of peasant origin, which kept to the tradition of work, order and reason." And the same was true of the world of business, in which those qualities of culture, education and status so regularly attributed to the French *citadin* were most often absent.

Even after spending a long time in the colonial environment, the French remained socially unsettled, not really belonging to the land or deeply wishing to be part of it. The one major exception was the *pieds noirs* of Algeria, who alone among the French colonial populations resembled the Boers of South Africa in their sense of settlement. Robert Delavignette in his *Service africain* assesses this general social ambivalence from the insider's perspective. Noting that the Europeans accounted for only a small part of the total population of the colonial territories—he says that in French West Africa between the wars there were 28,000 Europeans to 15,000,000 Africans—he concludes: "A minority in face of the native population, they [the Europeans] also are a minority in face of the populations at home. Europeans in the colony, they are colonials in metropolitan France." Much later, in 1951, the French sociologist Paul Mercier undertook a survey of the French population in Dakar and found that "none of the individuals interviewed had any desire to remain permanently in Africa."

In a way similar to the French, much of the "native" population in the colonial cities was not "native," but also colonial and transitory. Coming to the city in the hope of employment, perhaps to enhance their status at home, or to find the means to pay an *impôt personnel*, or to find a new kind of life, they left their own cultural environment principally to work temporarily on the wharves or in the tertiary sector of the economy. In Dakar, for instance, the basic Lebou element was joined by Tokolors, Fulani, Wolofs, and Moors, each element forming its own residential colony within the context of the city. The development of the port's naval facilities after 1898 was an important factor in attracting labor of an unskilled sort to Dakar. In Morocco, the Berbers moved northward to the growing urban centers, such as Fez, and competed with the Arabs in middle-level commerce. Similarly, along the west coast of Africa, the Syrio–Lebanese merchants began to make a striking appearance early in the twentieth century. In 1906 there were already 500 Syrio–Lebanese engaged in commerce in French Guinea, as compared with 350 Frenchmen and fewer than ninety other Europeans. In 1922 the Dakar Chamber of Commerce complained of the increased arrival of Syrio–Lebanese. "Each boat brings them in clusters. It's a true invasion against which we must struggle." Away from the African continent, the one group to appear in numbers more impressive than those of the Syrio–Lebanese was the Chinese. There were some 15,000 of them in Saigon in 1905, making up slightly more than a quarter of the population.

Demographic movement of this sort led to social discontent and agitation. As evidenced above, European merchants feared they would be overwhelmed by competition that could operate on a lower margin than they could. To the non-European populations that moved to the city, living conditions were distressing, employment often irregular and unsatisfactory. French observers spoke of the development of an urban proletariat in Dakar even before the war, while the city of Oujda in Morocco was a center of considerable proletarian unrest in the 1930s, when, having become industrialized, it was suffering from the effects of the European depression. Much of this economically precarious population settled in hastily constructed shanty towns or *bidonvilles*, as they were popularly called after World War II. There, domesticity was improvised amidst the most insanitary conditions and grave overcrowding. As late as 1951, only 5 per cent of the total population of Dakar had flush toilets, while the lack of paved streets and well-planned sewers in the "native quarters" meant flooding and typhoid conditions in the rainy season.

Not all of the indigenous population beckoned to the city endured these travails. An African and Asian bourgeoisie was a distinctive aspect of the interwar French colonial city. Not very numerous and not very wealthy, members of this newly-created class held minor administrative functions in the capital, edited some of the newspapers that were then appearing, owned cafés, entered colonial commerce, and taught in schools. There was a sprinkling of lawyers and of doctors as well. But, statistically, the rise of a significant indigenous bourgeoisie within the colonial framework occurred after World War II and with the increase of administrative services and the influx of new capital.

Visually as well as socially, the French colonial city was a study of contrasts. Wide, tree-lined boulevards and comfortable villas stood in defiance of dusty alleys and packing-box hovels. Newly imported typewriters kept a different cadence from the tom-toms which were heard nearby. The white-uniformed colonial sipping an aperitif at a sidewalk café was but a few meters away from the ragged leper begging for alms. And the statuesque Senegalese magnificently arrayed in a bright-colored boubou floated by the dully dressed Frenchwoman bringing home her purchases made at the central market.

Such cultural mosaics, daily displayed, were part of the general pattern of the city. Neither native to the region nor isolated from it, the colonial city was the port of entry for Frenchmen beginning colonial careers, and the point of departure for young Africans and Asians looking to a newer world, one in which they as a modern elite would stand next to the European—or perhaps replace him.

Whether sitting on a plateau or resting in the lowland of a delta, the French colonial city was a fixed monument to French colonial policy. Dr Anfreville de Salle, writing about Dakar in the June 15, 1912 issue of *La Revue*, commented, "It [Dakar] is a very recent undertaking, and therefore its study is of considerable interest, for in analysing this city, one can easily appreciate the qualities and shortcomings of our colonial methods." By extension, Anfreville's remarks could be applied to the urban development of the entire French empire.

Like the populations the colonial city housed and the services it

performed, a historical judgment of the success of French urbanization
in Asia and Africa must be mixed. Structurally, the urban scene was
quite impressive, the more so considering the inadequate funds available prior to World War II. Schools, hospitals, port facilities, streets
and sanitary services were of general benefit to the entire population,
and the provision of them was commendable. Attempts to grapple
with the vast problem of public housing were particularly laudable in
the terminal years of imperialism. But most of the improvements
were made from an assimilationist perspective: consideration of the
city as an extension of France. The result was that the strictly colonial
cities, such as Dakar, were inconsonant with indigenous needs or
interests; while older cities, upon which the French placed their urban
overlay, endured a sort of cultural trauma, because their religious or
administrative purposes were destroyed, their older quarters defiled
by modern engineering. Lastly, the colonial city was a responsible
agent for the process of "deruralization"—the demographic movement away from the countryside. Put conversely, the phenomenon of
overurbanization, of more urban dwellers than the city economy can
support, has been an unfortunately enduring one, with financial and
political strains that are obvious.

In the days of the Phoenicians and the Greeks, colony and city were
for all practical purposes synonymous terms; certainly, the former
was planned as an urban structure. Following that classical tradition,
the French have marked the coasts of Asia and Africa with cities that
still stand as concrete evidence of what the *mission civilisatrice* meant.

Chapter Six

From the Other Side

"You are not a torch, you are a fire. Everything you touch, you consume." In this statement, directed to colonial France and designed as a polemical preface to his novel *Batouala*, René Maran denied the major premise of French imperialist ideology. In so doing the black Martiniquan author shocked many of his readers and perhaps added a well-calculated irritant by couching this statement in the French familiar form of "you," a practice condescendingly used by the French with the "natives." However, the novel, concerned with African life as perceived through African eyes, was a single-volume literary revolution; it was awarded the coveted Goncourt prize in the year of its publication, 1921, and thus became the first book by a black author to be so honored. *Batouala* stands as a sort of manifesto, a protest against the then-current colonial situation and a statement reflecting the sentiment of many intellectuals in the French Empire.

The interwar period was a significant one in the history of the "third world," for at that time there appeared many expressions of discontent with colonial rule and many assertions of the dignity and richness of the cultures that the French seemed to ignore as they set about the business of colonial administration. Not many such works received the acclaim or caused the stir that Maran's novel did. Nonetheless, in places such as Saigon, Algiers and Tananarive, and even in Fort-de-France on Martinique, a new literature was generated by like-minded individuals asking that they be self-identified. Furthermore, this activity went beyond the cultural. If many of the movements were predominantly literary in purpose and romantic in tone, others were decidely political and potentially revolutionary. Although none shook empire or even deeply disturbed the complacency of most colonial administrators, some did erupt into activity that was serious enough to receive aggressive, even brutal, administrative response.

The most salient characteristic of all these movements was their youthful composition. In general, they were initiated by members of a generation that had made its appearance shortly before and after the war. The "Young Algerians," the "Young Tunisians," the "Christian Young People's Movement" in Madagascar, and the "Youth Party" in Vietnam were just some of the organizations that grew up in the colonial cities in the first two decades of the twentieth century. In inception none was pronouncedly nationalist in objective, but all were critical of French colonialism and most were particularly concerned with how their lands could adapt to the new conditions thrust upon them. They were therefore particularly "modernist," respectful of the technological benefits of French civilization and given to finding social and political amalgams of Western industrial civilization and local culture.

The appeal to other than the colonial model was understandable. Both Japan and Turkey, two states moving into the twentieth century on their own terms, suggested possible models of social development for the colonized peoples. In 1904 Phan Boi Chau, the most significant member of the new literary elite in Vietnam, undertook a trip to Japan, where he sought both aid and advice. He was soon disturbed by the signs of imperialism he saw there, but for other observers Japan was still to be admired from a distance. In a 1927 newspaper article, Ferhat Abbas, one of the most significant interwar intellectuals in Algeria, wrote, "Following the example of Japan, all the Arab peoples aspire to learn in the European school but without thereby renouncing their civilization and their traditions." The young Turk movement of the prewar era inspired the "Young Tunisians" and the "Young Algerians," as their names clearly indicate.

It was the World War, more than any other force, that accelerated these movements, as it displaced colonial populations, gave rise to new expectations and, at long range, caused the great depression, which unseated the colonial economies and thereby aggravated the colonial situation. The military efforts made by the colonial peoples, the rapid spread of a democratic idealism in the wake of victory, and the role played by certain non-European leaders, such as Prince Faisal of Arabia, in defeating the enemies of France all suggested to the colonial elites that an era of reform might be at hand. Moreover, individuals such as Sarraut promised as much.

Equally assuring were signs from within Europe. The colonial question was posed at the time of the Paris Peace Conference. W. E. B. DuBois, head of the National Association for the Advancement of Colored People and already active in the Pan-African movement, used the good offices of Blaise Diagne, the Senegalese representative in the French parliament, to persuade Clemenceau to allow the convening of a Pan-African conference. It met in February 1919 in the Grand Hotel in Paris and was composed of some fifty-seven delegates from the United States, the Caribbean, and West Africa. As DuBois wrote, "The results of the meeting were small." This was certainly true of the immediate outcome, but the effort to get the victorious colonial powers to reform their administration of Africa was a clear announcement that national policy henceforth had to take into account a growing international opinion. More demanding and denunciatory of the colonial powers was the 1927 Brussels Congress Against Imperialism and Colonial Oppression, marked by an impressive list of speakers, including Jawaharlal Nehru of India and Mohammed Hatta of Indonesia, and with the future nationalist leader in Algeria, Messali Hadj, in attendance. Within France itself, a growing literature of colonial inquiry suggested new national consciousness. The most famous of the works then appearing was, of course, André Gide's *Voyage au Congo*, a dossier of severe charges against the French colonial practices in Equatorial Africa and a journalistic experience that moved Gide toward communism. In 1935 Jean Melia wrote *Le Triste sort des indigènes musulmans en Algérie* an account strongly dissenting from the official view of social conditions in colonial Algeria. Also, the Comité de Vigilance des Intellectuelles Antifascistes, including the famous liberal-republican essayist Alain, issued a pamphlet in 1936 that argued in favor of the eventual freedom of all colonial peoples. Removed temporarily from the metropolitan scene, the then young and radical André Malraux was in Indochina in 1925 and 1926, where he was attempting to arouse an interest in colonial liberalization. In 1927 he published his first major work, *La Tentation de l'ouest*, a dialogue between a Frenchman and an oriental, with the latter having the best of the argument and thereby proving the pretentiousness of Western civilization.

Among French political parties, regardless of their particular ideological persuasion, there was no such strongly articulated and maintained opposition to imperialism. At best the parties vacillated in statement, hesitated in policy. The Radical Socialists, the center-republican party, were primarily represented by the thought of Albert Sarraut, who spelled out reform in broad terms of *mise en valeur*. The Socialists had arrived at a position of *juste milieu*. Their leading doctrinaire in the prewar period, Jean Jaurès, was in great part responsible for this attitude. He had declared that France's civilizing mission should not be discounted, even though he inveighed against the exploitative nature of capitalistic imperialism. In an article appearing in the May 17, 1897, edition of *La Petite république*, Jaurès summed up as follows his interpretation of the evils of imperialism: "The cunning ferocity of primitive humanity is [in the colonial situation] marvelously set to work by the ingenious mechanism of the capitalist machine." Condescending toward the colonized peoples, wary of the motives of the capitalist, Jaurès saw the state as having an important function to play as sponsor of public works beneficial to both the indigenous populations and France. In sum, he detested imperialism but counted on France's revolutionary humanitarianism to mollify the colonial situation. His successor to party leadership after the war was Léon Blum, who assumed an attitude similar to that of Jaurès's. In the matter of colonialism, as with so much of the ideology of French socialism, the myth of 1789 was larger than the Marxist myth: fraternity, not class warfare, was the key.

Of course the one political group that should unhesitatingly have sided with the colonial peoples was the newly-formed French Communist Party. Yet it did not prove to be truculently anti-imperialist. The official Soviet doctrine, based on Lenin's twenty-one points of 1921, was at first reluctantly accepted by the French party. However, in 1924 the party did take a vigorous stand on the Rif War in Morocco, urging support for the insurgents. Generally, politics dominated ideology, even in this most doctrinaire of modern French political parties. The dual obligation to court the votes of the metropolitan workers and to follow the vicissitudes of Soviet foreign policy made a consistent and forceful policy all but impossible. Indeed, by 1936, with the growing fascist threat and Russia's inclination, in European policy, toward the Western democracies, the French Communist Party assumed a rather moderate position on the colonial question.

1936 was, of course, the year of France's first Popular Front government, one that seemed to be well left-of-center, with its support derived from the Radical Socialists, Socialists, and Communists. Léon Blum assumed the Premiership, and Marius Moutet, a Socialist reformer and constant critic of colonial policy, was made Minister of Colonies. It was an inspiring moment for members of the colonial elite. Ferhat Abbas later gave voice to the sentiment of the time in his *Guerre et Révolution d'Algérie: La Nuite coloniale*, published in 1962: "Never was the Algerian people so unanimous in its hopes." But the Popular Front reforms, which on paper anticipated post-1945 enactments, came to little. The famous Blum–Viollette bill, prepared by Maurice Viollette, former Governor-General of Algeria, would have increased by a few tens of thousands the number of Algerians qualifying for French citizenship and thus would have liberalized rule in that colony. However, this assimilationist movement with severe opposition from the *colons* in Algeria and was, moreover, treated cautiously by Blum himself, aware as he was of the precarious hold his government then had on French politics.

The sum result of all this moderate political fermentation was negligible. Colonial policy continued much as before. Reflecting back on this time, Abbas pointed out with regret that the Centenary in Algeria, which Viollette had hoped would be an occasion for reform and the moment for a new rapport between French and Arabs, was more of the old show. "The army of 1830 was historically reconstructed and made to march through the streets of Algiers," he ruefully remarked. In similar manner, a statement made at the time to the effect that "the most perfect order and calm reigned" called forth from the Franco-Arab sociologist Jacques Berque, in his *Le Maghreb entre deux guerres*, the following response of: "Externally, this was true, yet the crowd murmured, it seems, when the Moslem delegation moved forward to greet the [French] visitors. What was felt in the depths of their hearts?"

Certainly heartfelt doubt was there, but it little disturbed the surface of Algerian or African affairs. French rhetoric expounded on the affection of the colonized peoples for the French effort down to the outbreak of the next war. In light of this complacency there is a strong temptation to repeat the old statement made about the early nineteenth century Bourbons and apply it to French colonial officialdom: they learned nothing, but they forgot nothing. To do so, however, would be historically distortive, simplistic. It must be remembered that in the interwar period the weakening position of France economically and politically, particularly at the very moment when the Popular Front government was entertaining its proposals for change, made any colonial reform unlikely of parliamentary success. In the age of Hitler, European affairs both predominated and enervated; and once again the fate of the French Empire was to be decided on the Rhine.

Conditions in Europe were of no immediate concern to the new elites within the colonial populations, who viewed the most pressing external problems as French in cause. Within the overseas territories, the interwar period was witness to expressions of protest, but France itself was the principal setting in which intellectual re-evaluation took place. Indeed, Paris emerged in the 1920s as the center of a new cosmopolitan world. Different faces and accents from all over the empire were seen and heard on the Left Bank, and they were joined by an impressive collection of self-described exiles from a Western world in cultural ferment. Nowhere was the empire freer than in Paris.

Two French developments brought considerable numbers of the colonized to the French capital. The first was the World War, and the second was government scholarships. Small groups from Vietnam, the Antilles, Algeria, and Black Africa gathered for debate in the cafés, edited brief-lived newspapers or small-circulation tracts, and attended rallies at the Salle Wagram, or in the small apartment of a favorite intellectual leader. Among their number were a former messboy on a French ocean liner, Nguyen Ai Quoc—later styled Ho Chi Minh; an Algerian laborer, Messali Hadj, who founded the Étoile Nord-africaine, the most radical anti-colonial movement in interwar French Africa; a young law student travelling on funds provided by his brother in 1924, Habib Bourguiba, who enjoyed the French theatre and literature of the day, and later became Life-President of Tunisia; a student at the École Normale Supérieure in the 1930s, Aimé Césaire, who founded the *négritude* school of poetry, and later represented Martinique in the French National Assembly; and an African student of French grammar, Léopold Sédar Senghor, who later achieved prominence as a poet and as President of Senegal.

In an atmosphere charged with new political developments, in the form of Wilsonian democracy and Leninist communism, and by new intellectual movements, such as surrealism and existentialism, the colonial immigrants were exhilarated at the thought of change and with the discovery of new cultural purpose. It was in this setting that Messali Hadj founded his anti-colonial proletarian movement Etole Nordafricaine (best known by its initials, *ENA*), which remained French-based until its intrusion into Algerian affairs in the middle 1930s. And it was also in this setting that many Vietnamese students debated the question of constitutional reform in their homeland and that the future Ho Chi Minh founded his ideology and vocation.

There is no doubt that Ho was one of the most dramatic and effective figures in Paris in the early 1920s. By all accounts he was a slight, delicate, ill-clothed personage who was also—and more significantly—an intense, indefatigible advocate of his nation's freedom. In collaboration with a fellow Vietnamese, he drew up, and hopefully presented to the Peace Conference for consideration, an eight-point program that imitated Wilson's Fourteen Points. He addressed the 1920 meeting of the French Socialist Party "as the Delegate from Indochina," and he impressed his auditors with his determination. Then Ho moved further left, as he voted that the Socialist Party join the Third International. The split this vote caused at the 1920 party convention at Tours led to the establishment of the French Communist Party, which counted Ho among its earliest members. Above all, Ho played the role of pamphleteer, writing particularly for *L'Humanité*, *Le Populaire*, and a short-lived anti-colonial journal, *Le Paria*. He also published, in 1923, *Le Procès de la colonisation*, a series of bitter articles covering the broad sweep of contemporary colonial issues. The work was a veritable indictment in which administrators and policies were roundly condemned. Perhaps the summary statement is the following: "It has been said that 'colonization is theft.' I say that it is theft and assassination."

Le Procès de la colonisation consisted of the most virulent comments to emerge at the time about the French Empire. Appropriately, shortly after their appearance, Nguyen Ai Quoc left Paris for Moscow. He was not missed in the general Parisian scene, which soon changed to present a tableau mounted by a different colonial element.

Of all the ethnic groups that gathered in interwar Paris, none was more culturally conscious, joyful in expression, hopeful about the future—and better received by the Parisian population—than these blacks from the Caribbean and West Africa. Indeed, from the French view of the colonial world, the black presence heralded a new era; it represented a new exoticism, and one situated right in the nation's capital. Several critics, both black students and Parisian journalists, attributed the Parisian enthusiasm for *le monde noir* to the 1931 Parisian International Colonial Exhibition and the representations it provided of Black Africa. This may have been the major factor; but cultural preconditioning reached back to the 1920s.

Postwar Paris, like Berlin, but in a less daring manner, gave vent to new forms of popular culture, in which an exciting outburst not dissimilar to the "Harlem Renaissance" took place. The success of Josephine Baker, a black American singer and dancer, in the music hall; the enthusiastic reception of the first *Anthologie nègre*, edited by the French journalist and poet Blaise Cendrars in 1921; the captivating sounds of the Caribbean *béguine* in the dance halls; and the newly-appreciated black musical idiom from the United States—all these wrought their effects. Speaking of the last development, and in so doing capturing something of the general mood, Langston Hughes, a black American poet and novelist, wrote in his autobiographical *The Big Sea*, "Blues in the rue Pigalle. Black and laughing, heartbreaking blues in the Paris dawn, sounding like a pulsebeat, moving the Mississippi."

In this general atmosphere, largely of their own creation, black students became aware of their *africainété* and gave first lyrical expression to what later would be called *négritude*, the ideology of blackness. Black culture triangulated in Paris. From the Caribbean there was the influence of the Haitian Renaissance—a literary development that was primarily a response to the American Marine invasion of 1915, and a turning back to African roots, as the title of its most important publication, *Les Griots*, suggests. More powerful was the current from

North America, the mood of the Harlem Renaissance. Léopold Sédar Senghor later remarked that he and others came under the influence of black American writers such as Claude MacKay, Langston Hughes, and Countee Cullen in a salon that was maintained by a young woman from Martinique, Andrée Nardal, who, with her sister, was active among the colonial students. The black-American influence had earlier moved in quite a different geographical direction, but not a cultural one. According to Étienne Léro, one of the most important Martiniquan poets in Paris at the time, "The wind which blew from America quickly cleansed our Antilles of the abortive fruits of a decaying culture. Langston Hughes and Claude MacKay, the two revolutionary poets, brought to us, marinated in red alcohol, the African love of life, the African joy of love, the African dream of death . . . ."

Sentiments of this sort were given form in various little magazines that briefly flourished in Paris—particularly during the International Colonial Exhibition, which precipitated, even if it did not directly inspire, them. *La Revue du monde noir, Revue indigène, Légitime défense,* and *Étudiant noir* were the prominent black publications. All were extremely ephemeral. The one with the broadest cultural purpose was *La Revue du monde noir*, a bilingual publication that lasted for six issues and published a variety of black authors from the United States, the Caribbean and Africa. The lead editorial announced as its far-reaching purpose that "the two hundred million individuals who constitute the Negro race . . . will form . . . a great Brotherhood, the forerunner of universal Democracy."

This pan-African spirit, the realization of a cultural world that was transoceanic, was the exciting idea that the black students in Paris then discovered. Here was an attitude that might be considered expressive of romantic nationalism, a return to the culture of the native soil, and to the dreams and the moods it nurtured. Certainly Senghor would later celebrate such thoughts in his poetry, just as the most important figure behind the *négritude* movement had done before World War II. Aimé Césaire wrote *Cahier d'un retour au pays natal*, a poem of epic proportions, in 1939. It was then generally ignored, but was deeply appreciated by the surrealist writer André Bréton. After the war, its author and the ideology his work fostered became famous. The "native land" to which Césaire was immediately returning was Martinique, after his completion of studies in Paris. But the return was deeper, more far-reaching than that: it was a return to a basic dignity and purpose denied the black, a return to African roots. As Césaire protests in the *Cahier*, "For it is not true that the work of man is finished, that we have nothing to do in the world. . . . no race has a monopoly on beauty, intelligence, strength, and there is room for all at the rendezvous of conquest ...."

Négritude, blackness, the poetic exaltation of a people and of a culture, was also an ideological attack on French imperialism, for it denied French claims to cultural superiority and demanded instead an equality of condition. As Senghor put it in the publication *Poésies* in 1945, "It was no longer a matter of inferiority or superiority, nor of antagonism, but of creative difference." The concept of *négritude* was created by temporary exiles both geographically and culturally removed from their home through the force of French imperialism and the allure of Paris.

As might be imagined, there were many people not acquainted with Paris who sensed a similar alienation, who felt themselves foreigners in their own land. The new colonial elites in the French-developed and controlled cities overseas wanted more authority and less oppression. They all railed against the *indigénat*, the separate system of legal procedure and penalties that the French imposed on the non-French in most of their empire. They disliked the taxes exacted from them, which seemed to bring them little benefit, and they were equally disturbed at the inequality of salary between a Frenchman and a African or Asian with comparable duties. As part of a new intelligentsia, they complained about press restrictions and inadequate education. The final, and most persistent, of their grievances concerned the political system. They denounced an arrangement in which they were made a political minority among an alien people whom they in fact greatly outnumbered.

Demands such as these appeared in a variety of forms: editorials in newly-founded newspapers, conversations with colonial officers, public declarations, and manifestos. Indeed, the written manifesto, the contemporary variation of the *cahier de doléance*, or list of grievances, was a familiar publication in the interwar colonial world. For instance, when the new, socialist Governor-General of Indochina, Alexandre Varennes, arrived in 1927, he was greeted by some 600 Vietnamese who handed him a *Cahier des voeux annamites*. In Algeria, the Emir Khaled, grandson of Abd-el-Kadir and formerly a French army captain, drew up a *cahier de revendications*, which he submitted to the Algerian government shortly after reforms were introduced by France in 1919. For his efforts at obtaining what in essence amounted to equal political treatment for Arabs, the Emir was exiled, in 1923.

The thought informing this new mood of social and political dissatisfaction was eclectic in origin, a sort of groundswell moving in two directions, from east and west. The important point is that it moved everywhere. Lamine Guèye, later Senegalese representative to the French parliament and founder of the Socialist Party in French West Africa between the wars, commented in his memoirs that "the name of the American black Booker T. Washington was as well known to us as if he had lived in our country." Police dossiers from Dakar in the 1920s show concern over the possible spread of Garveyism—the ideas of the Jamaican leader Marcus T. Garvey, who founded the Universal Negro Improvement Association and who played a dominant role in the American black community of the 1920s. Vietnamese protesters assimilated some of the ideas of the late nineteenth century Chinese reformer Ch'i-ch'ao and watched with interest Sun Yat-sen's efforts to create a viable Chinese republic in European fashion in the early twentieth century. Nguyen An Ninh, editor of the widely-read Saigon newspaper *Cloche fêlée* and a strong advocate of Vietnamese constitutional reform, had, while a student in Paris, in 1918–20, translated Rousseau into *quoc-ngu*, thus making that political thinker available to a new generation of Vietnamese. And Lenin, of course, proved to export well, eventually even better than Woodrow Wilson, although the French form of republicanism, bathed in the revolutionary Jacobin tradition, was the most respected and most widely imitated at this time.

Of equal interest and to greater immediate effect was the use of activitist political tactics, some of a calculated and conspiratorial sort, others more spontaneous. The most singular fact about them is that they were not geographically restricted, but phenomena that occurred throughout the colonial empire. By way of a small political *tour du monde colonial*, consider the following instances. In 1912, a boycott of the tramlines of the city of Tunis, undertaken because of salary differentials and inconsiderate treatment of Tunisian customers, was supported by the Young Tunisians. Even though they had not initiated the boycott, four members of the Young Tunisian leadership were then deported by the colonial authorities. On May 20, 1914, 1,500 Lebous gathered before the town hall of Dakar to protest at what they considered discriminatory treatment in the French handling of the bubonic plague then besieging the city. Late in 1915 the French colonial administration on Madagascar feared an armed plot, supposedly scheduled for January 1916, to overthrow the regime. This danger was attributed to a secret society, the Vy Vato Sakelike, a militant and nationalistically-oriented outgrowth of the Christian Young People's Movement. In December 1915, some 500 Malagasy were accordingly arrested. In the summer of 1924 a member of a group of Vietnamese radicals then studying at the Whampoa Military Academy in Canton, China, attempted to assassinate Governor-General Jean Merlin, who was passing through the city on his way to Indochina. And in 1925 a series of riots occurred in Dahomey, on the west coast of Africa, over an increase in the local head tax. A state of siege was declared, and the military were called in to restore order.

The upheaval that would seem to have made the strongest impression on the French press and colonial administration was that which erupted at the Yen Bey Garrison in Tonkin in 1930. There, as in other military outposts, the recently formed Vietnam Quoc Dan Dang party—the Vietnamese Nationalist Party—had waged a program of political infiltration with the purpose of widespread revolt. The radical wing of the party had recently been frustrated by French political repression and considered action an imperative. It therefore planned a combined operation, with a series of garrison uprisings in Tonkin to be supported by assaults on Hanoi and Haiphong by party militia. Early in the morning of February 9, 1930, the planned revolt took place, but in an erratic and incomplete fashion, owing to confused orders and hesitancy upon the part of the conspirators. The Yen Bey garrison, the first to revolt and the one in which the most significant action took place, was quickly subdued by the French and the country was soon brought back to tense calm. The implications of this ill-tied nationalist action were not easily dismissed, however. If Indochina was the plum of the colonial service, it was also becoming the main seedbed of colonial opposition.

Along with such nationalist expressions of protest went an equally modern form, the strike, use of which was most apparent in the transportation system, which had been so quickly expanded just before the war. In 1924 a series of strikes broke out among the dock workers in Tunisia. These were given some direction and support by one Mohammed Ali, who was influential in the creation of the first indigenous Tunisian labor union, the Confédération des Travailleurs Tunisiens, which began life in December 1924 but soon after collapsed through French pressure. For his role as labor agitator and organizer, Ali was exiled for ten years. In Madagascar, Malagasy dockers in the port of Tamatave went on strike in 1925, but labor there did not begin to be organized until just before World War II, when Ravoahangy, former leader of the Vy Vato Sakelike movement of 1916, set up a number of small unions with the support of the French Confédération Générale du Travail. Railroads were also the scene of labor disputes. In 1925 the workers on the Dakar–St Louis railroad in Senegal staged a strike, and in 1929 so did the railroad workers in Vinh, Indochina.

Certainly, it is true that it was not until after 1945 that effective labor organization became a salient characteristic of anti-colonialism, but as early as the 1920s the effects of the capitalization of the economy and the creation of a global trade grid were generating the conditions for the emergence of a proletariat that would respond in a manner already familiar in metropolitan France. It would appear that Sarraut's longed-for *mise en valeur* was producing unintended and clearly unwanted effects.

"Modernists" throughout the French Empire were regularly using European methods of political protest and the words of European thinkers to support their political arguments. Even though the new generation were often militantly proud of their own intellectual tradition, they consciously imitated—perhaps the word "imported" would serve better—techniques and thought that would, in effect, ricochet back on the French. The interwar period can therefore be described as the era in which political protest generally was expressed in terms of Western democracy. Ho Chi Minh admitted with a rather charming candor that in 1921, when he first became politically involved in France, "I understood neither what was a party, a trade-union, nor what was socialism and communism." Some thirty years later, in 1954, Hedi Nouira, a member of Tunisia's Neo-Destour Party, the principal agency of nationalist politics, commented that the party leaders had "borrowed their tactics, their organization, and their slogans from French political parties."

Of course the political evolution clearly implied in these two quotations did not occur in neat stages, anymore than it occurred with linear symmetry across the empire. Beyond the general characteristics that have so far been described, local cultures and traditions, the nature of French colonial involvement, and the structure of indigenous leadership all were mixed to create different historical responses. On a political scale running from left to right, from severe to moderate forms of protest, Vietnam would appear first, North Africa next, than Black Africa at the other end. Were there a device to measure intensity of protest, only Indochina would regularly show up, for resistance and expressions of discontent ran deeply through the entire history of French colonial rule there. Elsewhere, opposition was not so constantly registered and often was unnoticed in view of the outer appearance of public acquiescence in the colonial act.

Furthermore, enunciated opinion was far from being totally negative. In Madagascar and Black Africa there were few organizations as extreme as the generality of modern nationalist political parties. Indeed, there, as earlier in Indochina or Tunisia, major demands were for political assimilation, not independence. Blaise Diagne, the most influential black in French Africa in this period, said in 1922, "We blacks want to remain French, France having given us every liberty ...." In 1927 the Tananarive newspaper *L'Aurore malgache*, jointly edited by a Frenchman and two Malagasy patriots, sparked a move-

ment aimed at securing for the Malagasy the rights of French citizenship. Even Ferhat Abbas, active in Algerian protest movements,
suggested, in a famous and frequently cited statement made in 1936,
the appeal that political assimilation could still muster. Arguing that
an Algerian nation had not existed in historical fact, he concluded,
"We have therefore pushed aside all clouds and [nationalist] dreams in
order to tie our future definitely to the French achievement in this
country."

The French gladly accepted these words of praise and even
assumed that they represented widespread sentiment. Of course they
did not—no more than the incipient nationalist movements of the time
could be labelled "popular." Both the pro-French elite and the anti-
colonial elite were tiny minorities in territories populated by peoples
weighted down by the traditions, problems, and beliefs of centuries.
What is important, however, is that these political minorities faced the
other political minority, the French colonial administration and the
colons, who were as often divided as united on the policy to be
followed.

Because they were minority groups, frequently separated geographically and also often forced to clandestine activity, the anti-
colonial elites heavily depended on dedicated leadership. Habib Bourguiba, leader of the Neo-Destour Party, stated in 1954, "It is rare that
the events that make up the landmarks in the life of one man are
integrated into the history of a people to such an extent that the man
seems to incarnate his whole people." Perhaps it can be argued that the
situation in the colonial world was not so rare as Bourguiba would
have it. The young generation of the 1920s lived to become the old
fathers of the new nation-states. That messboy who went under the
name of "Ba" while on shipboard lived long enough to be called,
affectionately, "Uncle Ho." Senghor, a young student in the Paris of
the 1930s, is today still President of the Republic of Senegal. And
Messali Hadj, whose role in Algerian affairs was never so dominant, at
least remained influential in indigenous political development until
1954 and the outbreak of the national liberation movement. In sum,
this was quite an unusual generation, whose lives, chronologically as
well as politically, paralleled the change in status from imperialism to
national independence. The quality and duration of the dominant
personality therefore counted as much, in the early anti-colonial
movements, as did the ideological program.

To make such an assertion is not to discount ideology. Certainly it
was an extremely important factor in most instances, for it had to face
old values and, therefore, either integrate or displace them. In no other
region was this problem more obvious than in North Africa, where

Islam as a cultural system, not only a religion, was placed in conflict with French colonialism, viewed as a rival cultural system. Indeed, the reaction in the immediate postwar era was much the same in all three French states of the Maghreb: defensive and conservative. In Morocco the Salafiyya movement, a reformist movement seeking purification by return to the old faith, the old values, was dominant. Only when the old culture was well conserved could adaptation to Western ideas be considered, ran the general dictum. Of a similar order was the Algerian Association of Reformist Ulama, founded in 1931. It too stood in defiance of Western culture and for the revitalization of Islam. Finally, in Tunisia, there was a conservative quality to the Destour Party, which replaced the Young Tunisians in the interwar period. Its membership came from the traditional sectors of Tunisian society, and its vision was of a Tunisia before colonization: noble, efficient, good—and, of course, unhistorical.

Ultimately more important were the more radical groups that made an appearance in certain sectors of the empire. They were decidedly nationalist, often left of center, and generally activist. And because of their radical position *vis-à-vis* colonialism, their leadership was frequently forced to reside in exile, as Ho Chi Minh did during most of the 1930s, or endure prison sentences, as Habib Bourguiba and Messali Hadj did—and, as a matter of fact, as Ho did in 1931, at the hands of the British in Singapore. One further point merits mention: whether they were "charismatic" figures or not, most of these leaders were persuasive speakers and writers. There is general agreement about Bourguiba's excellence as an orator. As for Ho Chi Minh, while he was in Paris he worked to overcome a tendency toward lisping and an outwardly unforceful manner. Furthermore, to make his writings effective, he struggled to gain—and succeeded in gaining—a mastery of French written form.

Few would doubt that Ho Chi Minh was the most significant of the nationalist leaders to appear at this time. Accounts provided by a French Communist Party leader and by a member of the French Sûreté who was placed to watch his activities attest to his dedication and intellectual fervor. After encountering Leninism for the first time, in Paris, he never deviated from it, and the fact that he made it the main pillar of faith of the nationalist movement in Indochina caused him to be hunted by the French. Although some debate exists over the circumstances of the founding of the Indochinese Communist Party, the party did appear in 1929, and Ho provided it with a manifesto of objectives in 1930. The first objective was "to overthrow French imperialism, feudalism, and the reactionary capitalistic class." The party played cat-and-mouse with the French authorities and it was only during the brief Popular Front era that it was allowed freedom to organize. Then, it, along with the Socialists, amassed tens of thousands of demonstrators to celebrate May Day in Hanoi in 1938.

Though Ho came to be the principal figure associated with Indochina's "wars of liberation," first against the French and later against the Americans, historically he stands at the end of a line of leaders and movements that stretches back to the first years of French imperialism in the region. In truth, no French possession rested so uneasily under foreign rule as did Vietnam. Hardly had the French tipped the scale in their military conquest of Tonkin than the Emperor of Annam issued his famous edict of July 13, 1885, the Can Vuong, in which he pleaded with the scholar-gentry of the land to continue the struggle against the invader. This resulted in the emergence of the Can Vuong movement, which was both literary and activist, presenting the French with an annoying military problem in the north. After the turn of the century and the collapse of the Can Vuong movement, Indochinese resistance gravitated around the person of Phan Boi Chau, who turned to Japan for support and arranged for students to go there to be trained as part of a new generation of resisters. Phan first fostered a Modernization Society designed to reform the Annamite monarchy, but after Sun Yat-Sen's revolution of 1911 he created a Restoration Society, with republicanism as its objective. In the first years of the interwar period, the most obvious figure on the political scene was Nguyen An Ninh, editor of the *Cloche fêlée*. He was bent on the modernization of Vietnamese society, but grew ever more doubtful that this could be achieved under French rule. Then, in the years 1925–7, the Vietnam Quoc Dan Dang party (associated with the Yen Bey garrison uprising) was formed.

This brief résumé, all too rapidly and sweepingly passing over a rich and complicated history of nationalist protest, serves no other purpose than to suggest the unique political position of Indochina in the anti-colonial movements the French were seriously observing and soon, after World War II had upset all the old colonial balances of power, would be desperately facing. No other French-held territory was so agitated—perhaps another reason, but certainly not one that would have been advertised, for accepting the frequent comparisons the French have made between British India and French Indochina.

In North Africa, too, expressions of discontent would have registered (although more moderately) on a political seismograph. In the 1930s a new activist element appeared in Algeria, where there had been little visible political agitation since the 1870s. The failure of the Blum–Viollette bill, on which many Algerians had pinned high hopes, was a source of grave disappointment. A few years earlier, a Federation of Elected Moslems, in which Ferhat Abbas was a significant figure, was organized to speak for the still grossly-underpresented Moslems in the Algerian council. After 1936, Messali Hadj's Étoile Nordafricaine appeared in Algeria under a slightly different name. Outlawed both in France and Algeria, the party grew in influence, despite its nominal changes; it ended up as the Parti du Peuple Algerienne in 1939, but was once again outlawed, with Hadj then sent to prison.

Probably no figure was more prominent in interwar North Africa than Habib Bourguiba. Educated in Paris, a lawyer by training and a journalist by profession, in 1932 he began the journal *Action tunisienne*. From this and those associated with it developed the Neo-Destour Party, which officially came into existence on May 2, 1934. Bourguiba himself had admitted that he was no doctrinaire, rather a tactician. Nevertheless, he would not compromise or combine with the old Destour Party, which he and his followers had defeated in a party congress. Pointing toward a modern secular state, employing political tactics that were mostly French in derivation, he seized upon those issues that were of momentary importance and thus immediately important to the success of his nationalist movement. The example often given of this particular tactic is his urging the Tunisian people not to pay taxes during the lean years of the great depression.

The French authorities viewed Bourguiba with concern, considering him revolutionary and a threat to the public peace. He was given a second jail sentence in 1938, after two years of political freedom; and so, at the very end of the interwar period, shortly before the French nation found greater problems to worry over, he joined Messali Hadj away from the colonial political scene.

Certainly the France of 1939 had none of the confidence or military enthusiasm that had characterized the nation in 1914. Yet concern over the condition of the empire was no more profound than it had been in 1914. True, there was some uneasiness, particularly about Indochina and Tunisia, but these other shores quickly receded from view as the Nazi menace rose over the European continent. When war broke out, colonial troops again joined the French on the Western Front. And they, too, were imprisoned when, before long, the Germans overran the land. Léopold Sédar Senghor was among them—and so were many Africans who would prove far less illustrious than he would. Defeat came suddenly and surprisingly, engulfing colonizer and colonized alike.

Yet only two years before, on the occasion of the Parisian International Exposition of 1937, the world was not so grim in appearance that the artist for the popular magazine *Illustration* had to forgo painting pleasing water-colors of the various colonial buildings at the exposition. All the colonial territories were represented there, their varying pavilions being grouped together on the "Island of Swans" in the middle of the Seine. This small parcel of land, some 8,000 square meters in size, had been enlarged, through the use of pylons, to a size of 32,000 square meters. It may thus be considered the final act of French colonial expansion, and one played out in the shadow of the Eiffel Tower. The more romantic approach to this never-never world constructed there was made by gondola. Here was the last delightful fantasy that the French created for their global colonial empire.

Chapter Seven

The Retreat from Empire

There is general agreement among historians that the colonial era
came to an end in 1939, even though the façade and ritual of empire
continued well into the middle of this century. "Decolonization" was
a political phenomenon principally of, the 1950s and 1960s, but it was
in the war decade that the old colonial situation was irretrievably lost,
with worldwide events shattering the grandest of illusions and
weakening the strongest of institutions.

Put otherwise, a new global age was brutally introduced by World
War II, and in it there was no secure place for the colonial empires,
which were an outgrowth of Europe's earlier international paramountcy. No more easily appreciated indication of the upsetting of
the old balance of power is to be found than the following brief
statistical statement: not a single European colonial power escaped
scathing defeat on the world scene, and all—save Great Britain—
endured defeat in their homelands. Empire, made by the sword and
maintained by the sword, was blown apart by the weapons of modern
war. And so the appearance of European military supremacy was
quickly dissipated, and, as it vanished, the emblems of empire were
seen to be false. Paul Mus, General de Gaulle's representative to the
resistance movements in Indochina and later a professor at the Collège
de France, remarked that when the French returned to Hanoi they
should have grasped the meaning behind the fact that the larger-than-
life statue of Paul Bert, onetime governor, had already been over-
turned.

The French condition of empire was unique, even in this age of
global levelling. In June 1940 France endured a devastating and
"strange defeat," so sudden and complete that the basic political fabric
of the nation was rent. By the terms of the imposed German armistice,

a French satellite state, commonly known as the Vichy Regime, ruled the two-fifths of the nation yet unoccupied by German troops. However, another French nation came into being, a nation of the airwaves, commanded by the stentorian voice of General Charles De Gaulle. De Gaulle took to the radio from London on the evening of June 18, 1940, the day after France sought peace terms. He then made his famous declaration that France would fight on. "France is not alone!" he cried. "She is not alone! She is not alone! She has a vast empire behind her."

In August of this bleak summer of 1940, General De Gaulle was already looking around the expanses of that empire and seeking some promising political opportunity. He found it in French Equatorial Africa. Not only had there been, in this colonial region, popular demonstrations of discontent with the armistice, but, in addition, the Governor of Chad, Félix Eboué, had already indicated to De Gaulle in July that he was preparing to rally to the General's side. An improvised task-force of sorts, consisting of political leaders and a few military men, was selected by De Gaulle and then dispatched on British aircraft to begin negotiations and to undertake those maneuvers necessary for a transfer of power. The sum of their effort was a bloodless conversion of allegiance to the Free French, a movement at this time consisting, in Winston Churchill's words, of "General De Gaulle with only an unconquerable heart and a few kindred spirits." But the outcome was quick and remarkable. Eboué declared on August 16; Commandant Hautecloque—better known by his *nom de guerre*, Leclerc—took over Douala, capital of Cameroon, on August 17. Then Brazzaville changed hands on August 28; and the Governor of Oubangui announced his support as soon as he had news of the events in Brazzaville. Only Gabon held out, this ocean-front colony having been hastily reinforced by Vichy.

This successful Gaullist activity was followed, early in September, by expressions of allegiance from the French colonies in Oceania, the French coastal stations in India, and the islands of Saint-Pierre and Miquelon. The only attempted action that then went amiss was a naval bombardment of Dakar, designed to reduce the small Vichy naval force there, and to prepare for the take-over of French West Africa. In his *Mémoires*, De Gaulle said that this failure in September made him feel like a man whose house had fallen in on him during an earthquake.

Of course, that was a dramatic, personal reaction, not a strategic assessment. The failed naval expedition meant a great deal to De Gaulle but little to the global war situation—and not as much to the French Empire as activities that were occurring elsewhere. The North African campaign of 1941–2, made famous as a grand duel between Rommel and Montgomery, eventually led to Rommel's retreat into

Tunisia and to a series of severe battles that scarred that territory and shook French authority. To the west, the joint British–American invasion of Morocco and Algeria in November 1942 turned into a major military confrontation with Vichy forces. However, after politically expedient negotiations with the Vichy leader then in Algeria, the Allies obtained French support, so that a precarious peace thereafter reigned. By the early autumn of 1943 General De Gaulle had risen to be the most important figure in French North African politics even though he had first been excluded from operations in the region by the Allies, who had doubted everything about him but his wilfulness. His provisional government was established in Algeria, thus for a brief moment making the empire the seat of French authority.

Elsewhere the colonial war developments may not have been so dramatic, grand-scaled, or politically complicated, but they did suggest the further disruption of French imperial rule. In point of fact, these overseas developments could not have begun more dismally in 1940 if they had been contrived by a classical Greek dramatist. On the eve of total defeat in France, the *Massilia*, the ship carrying the members of the intended government-in-exile, was held up in Casablanca harbor and then forced, by order of Marshal Pétain, to return to France. And so the Third Republic collapsed in France; it did not continue in Africa. Shortly thereafter, on July 3, an extremely disturbing blow was administered to the already-shattered French national psyche, this time by the British. Under orders of Winston Churchill, a naval squadron appeared off Algeria and gave an ultimatum to the French naval units harbored at Mers-el-Kabir. They were given the alternatives of surrendering, of proceeding to a port secure from Nazi power, or of succumbing to destruction. The last was the solution rendered, for the French proved recalcitrant. In the ensuing gunfire, the fourth greatest naval establishment in the world foundered in Algerian coastal waters.

Throughout the war years the French Empire was militarily rearranged. In July 1941, joint British–French military action brought Syria and Lebanon under Gaullist control. In May 1942, a British naval force landed at Diego Suarez Bay in Madagascar, then stumbled on land in a Gallipoli-like campaign, but subdued the Vichy forces there in a few days. The Vichy-French situation in Indochina was not so violently altered. However, French rule was quickly reduced to acquiescence to Japanese demands. The Japanese established their military in the territory and only suffered continued French rule. But in March 1945, when collapse of the Japanese Empire seemed imminent, the French were removed from power altogether, large numbers were imprisoned, and a puppet state ruled by the Annamite Emperor,

Bao Dai, was declared independent. The combination of these actions, to which must be added the increased efforts of Ho Chi Minh, made the French situation there untenable, never again to be secured.

Far removed from all such military difficulties, in the idyllic setting of Martinique, in the Caribbean, the French aircraft-carrier *Jeanne d'Arc* waited out the war at anchor. Aside from assuring Vichy rule on the island, which counted not at all in the war, this large naval vessel's only use was symbolic; it was an impressive form of French imperial impotence.

Viewed from any angle, the French colonial scene was in disarray in the years 1940–5. Contending Free French and Vichy authorities engaged in military scuffles that had the characteristics of civil war; foreign occupation discredited French rule and often brought its own anti-colonial ideology; liberation of much colonial territory by the Americans, and to a lesser degree by the British, raised the hope that the colonial era might soon be replaced by a more democratic one. Everywhere, regardless of action and response, French weakness was nakedly revealed. The recovery of the confidence, the determination, and the ability to rule an empire was badly, perhaps hopelessly, impeded by a war that cruelly proved that France was no longer a great power.

In face of this gloomy situation stood General De Gaulle, already deeply appreciative of the political base France's African territories had provided him—and already convinced that France's postwar global role, the nation's redefinition of *grandeur*, would in large measure depend on the restitution of the empire. De Gaulle looked forward, and with some hope. In his *Mémoires*, he describes this vision of the future as imagined in 1940: "National liberation, if it were one day accomplished thanks to the forces of the Empire, would establish between France and the overseas territories lines of community." An attempt to define these lines was made at the most significant wartime colonial conference—indeed, the most significant French colonial conference in the twentieth century.

At Brazzaville in January 1944, officials from all of the African territories met to discuss and organize the future of the empire. While their ideological approach was not significantly new, their intentions were. They began with a familiar general premise which appeared in their final report as a statement now famous by frequent citation:

> The aims of the civilizing effort accomplished by France in her colonies rules out any idea of autonomy, any possibility of evolution outside the French bloc of empire; the eventual

or even the ultimate institution of self-government must be avoided.

In other words, the imperialist structure would remain essentially what it had been—directed to integration, not dissolution. But, though the general framework was seen as undergoing little alteration, there was an inclination towards greater autonomy for the colonial territories. In this matter the most striking proposal was for elected local or territorial assemblies with some responsibility for budgetary and administrative matters. In principle old colonial rule would give way to new cooperative administration, but ultimate control of all major political matters would rest in Paris. Even there, however, some change was envisaged. It was suggested that the colonial territories should have a greater say in the activities of the national government, through the creation of a "colonial parliament" or perhaps of a "federal assembly," in which colonial representatives would join the French.

A number of non-political matters were also considered. Proposals for increased educational opportunities, economic improvement by way of investment and development, and removal of the infamous *indigénat* were put forward. In sum, the relationship between colonizer and colonized on the territorial level would be drastically altered in law and in fact. However, all such reforms were necessarily delayed, for the Brazzaville Conference had no elected authority; it was the creation of a provisional government with no constitutional power of its own. Only when France had re-established its own legitimate government could colonial reform be undertaken.

As most critics have observed, the Brazzaville Conference demonstrated a willingness to undertake revision, to reconsider the nature of French imperial rule. In his opening address to the conference, General De Gaulle acknowledged the need for change. "At the moment that the present world war began," he stated, "there already appeared the necessity to restructure the development of our Africa, of the human progress of its inhabitants, and of the exercise of French sovereignty." But the restructuring was essentially of a local, administrative sort that would not greatly alter the general form of the French Empire. De Gaulle and his immediate advisors, like the governments that would soon follow them, worked on the assumption that liberalization, not fundamental reconstitution, would satisfy new demands, would channel intensifying political energies. No one yet had the desire, the courage, the wisdom—or the telescopic vision—to see a world in which an extended France, an overseas France, did not exist.

It is an irony of French colonial history that the empire took on its greatest national meaning at the time of its terminal decline. The tenacity with which the French held on to its crumbling units suggests that this intelligent people did not recognize the logic of necessity. No political party, even the Socialist or the Communist, wished to whittle away French sovereignty overseas, although their reasons did not always coincide with De Gaulle's concept of *grandeur*.

Largely as a result of this general attitude, the French Empire was thereafter treated like some old country chateau that its owners found beyond their means to maintain, but that remained a magnificent property and seemed to merit repairs in those parts that still appeared structurally sound.

In more prosaic terms, the empire was revised on paper.

In the course of the deliberations in late 1945 and 1946 over the constitutional form that the Fourth Republic should take, considerable discussion was devoted to the overseas territories. Both colonizers and colonized took this activity seriously, but each group had a different vision of what the future should hold.

On one matter there was agreement. The old empire should not be reconstituted. The new term "French Union" already indicated a nominal difference. "Union," of course, had something of a federal ring to it, as witness the word's long use in American history, or its particular connotation in the German *Zollverein*, customs union, a nineteenth century development considered a major step toward German unification. But precisely how the new French Union should be constituted was a question hotly disputed and disappointingly resolved. The result was a compromise more in keeping with the politics of the Third Republic than with the spirit of "national regeneration" that supposedly informed the thought and purposes of Frenchmen in the immediate postwar era.

Beyond the name, the French Union formally altered the administrative structure of empire. First, the Union consisted of three constituent parts: France itself, and then the colonial possessions, either departments or territories. To these were added the "Associated States," the two North African protectorates and possibly Indochina, whose status at the time was confused. The Union would have a High Council, to which the Associated States would send appointed representatives; and it would also have an Assembly, to which each of the colonies would send elected representatives, the total number of which would be one-half of the Assembly's membership, the other half coming from France itself. As the Assembly was only an advisory body, any high hopes that the colonial elite may have had for a more pronounced role in imperial administration were dashed. The old parliamentary system, now styled the National Assembly, still controlled overseas affairs; and, even though it received an increased number of colonial representatives, the French were still in the majority. Behind it all was the fearful concern of the old republican politician Édouard Herriot that, if the overseas territories were represented on exactly the same terms as France, France would become a colony of its colonies.

Perhaps more important than any of the final provisions structuring the French Union was the disillusionment of the colonial delegates. Algerians and Malagasy were angry that their requests for independence were not seriously considered. Indeed, an original provision which stipulated that membership of the Union ought to be voluntary was rejected. African delegates anticipating increased democracy in the form of local assemblies, as considered at the Brazzaville Conference, were sorely disappointed. The law allowing for such assemblies was part of the first draft constitution; but it did not appear in the second, which was the voted one. Even as the constitutional convention ended its work, colonial figures were decrying the Union as a farce and a sham.

Their complaints proved to be more accurate than false. Whatever the intentions of the French involved in its establishment, as a system of colonial rule the Union failed, owing to its administrative clumsiness and its inability to take account of rapidly changing conditions overseas. The one major effort at reform within the Union structure was the Defferre Law, named after the Minister of Overseas France who proposed it in 1956. This enactment finally realized the long-discussed idea of responsible territorial assemblies for Africa. Here indeed was a genuine effort at decentralization and at devolving political power to local, elected representatives. True, it may not have been quite as noble as it looked, for it did lead to the decline of federal colonial authority in Africa and thus seemed to prepare for what Léopold Senghor called the "balkanization of West Africa." Yet this reform was too late to have any significant impact on the shape of empire.

By 1956, the year in which the Defferre Law was enacted, the only major territories of the empire that were not irretrievably lost were in sub-Saharan Africa. Elsewhere independence had already occurred, as in Indochina, or severe resistance to the French was taking place, as in Algeria. Indeed, the only postwar French colonial effort that seemed to have continuing success was found in the field of economics and concentrated in sub-Saharan Africa.

In 1946 the French government introduced a plan for economic development. This, the Fund for Economic and Social Development—known best by its acronym, FIDES—was financed mainly by the national budget, with the bulk of its money being employed to enlarge the communications systems and to enhance urban construction in Africa. However, the funds were never sufficient to keep up with increasing demands, particularly for consumer industries and for such basic services as cheap public housing. And so, in the end, FIDES was rushed along by the African wind of change. It was really Albert Sarraut's *mise en valeur*, a war and a revolution too late—to use an expression coined by Ferhat Abbas.

In these years of colonial collapse, there seemed time for only one more major institutional change. That occurred in the dark days of the Algerian troubles, which brought about the disintegration of the Fourth Republic and the recall of General De Gaulle from private life to the forefront of French politics. De Gaulle's dream of a restored empire was now gone. What he hoped to do in the present situation was to avert another Algeria in Black Africa, the only mass of territory still somewhat secure in French hands, but obviously soon to slip away.

De Gaulle's chief mission was to save France from political chaos, and to do this clearly required the final devolution of empire. A new constitution was the immediate order of business, one that would strengthen France at home and abroad. Deliberations over the future status of the African possessions were undertaken by a special consultative committee, whose membership soon formed into two loose factions, one considering a possible federal arrangement, the other seeking something still vaguer and looser in terms of confederation. The committee was particularly anxious to avoid rigid definition, and thus to assure the adjustment of the new imperial relationship to the rapidly changing world conditions. It was the representative from Madagascar, Philibert Tsiranana, who hit upon the metaphysical solution that seemed to be required. He suggested that a "Community" be established.

Though the name had already been incorporated into French political language by General De Gaulle, the proposed structure was at severe variance with all that had preceded it. The Community was to be an umbrella of services—such as common foreign affairs, defense, and finances—beneath which individuality, the activities of "Free States," would be protected. In the words of the Keeper of the Seal who explained the project to the General Constituent Assembly, "There is no parliamentary system arranged for this organization; rather it is a regime founded on the collegial authority of the responsible politicians of each state, with a supreme arbiter who is the President of the Community . . . ."

Although the final arrangements were hardly so unstructured and simple as just described, they did constitute a deviation from previous models. There would be a President; a Council of the Community, acting as a sort of super-cabinet; and a Senate, but with advisory powers only. The system was ill defined; but this was an academic matter, for the Community was never fully realized. In less than a year-and-a-half, it had entered that detailed French history of shelved or short-lived constitutions.

However, this was not because of a lack of effort on De Gaulle's part. In the month before the constitutional referendum was to take place, between August 20 and September 28, the General made a grand tour of Black Africa, a tour that was a personal triumph and an indication that the Community idea might succeed. And so it did briefly. Only Guinea voted against in the referendum; elsewhere the success was magnificent, with 89.8% of the voters in the overseas departments—such as Martinique and Guadeloupe—voting in favor. Nonetheless, this electoral victory was illusory. By 1960 all of the major African territories had achieved independence, and all that was left of the French overseas empire were a few coastal and island remnants.

The historical truth is that even the political adroitness of De Gaulle could not compete with the changes of the times. Colonial empire, whatever its form and however generous the spirit which animated its alteration, no longer had a place in the contemporary world. Moreover, what was crystal clear in 1958, when the Community was founded, could have been discerned a good decade before.

The war years proved to be a rather propitious time for the reform and independence movements emerging within the empire. Yet no simple indirect ratio of declining colonial power and rising national resistance can be historically posited. The process of change was more complicated and erratic than that—at times quick and peaceful, at other times slow and destructive. One thing was certain: the number of newly defined parties of protest was discernibly increasing and making bolder demands.

The strongest opposition was in Indochina and North Africa, the areas in which French rule had been most badly eroded. In May 1941, Ho Chi Minh, once again in Indochina, established the Viet Minh, or League for Vietnamese Independence, in what was surely the most bucolic setting in which any such movement has been born. Amidst the lush countryside of northern Vietnam, within a hastily constructed hut, and around a bamboo table—all removed from French and Japanese eyes—the members of the Indochinese Communist Party formed the League, which was immediately dedicated to the overthrow of

French and Japanese imperialism and, in turn, to the establishment of a democratic Vietnamese republic.

In North Africa, the shifting fortunes of war made 1943 a premium year for the formation of several new activist groups and the enunciation of new demands. The American presence was certainly a contributing factor, but so also was that of the Free French, who appeared representative of a new order. What almost had the form of a set sequence of events began in February, when Ferhat Abbas issued a "Manifesto of the Algerian People," in which he demanded for the country internal self-determination and recognition of Moslem authority, though within the framework of a "French federation." Abbas's new position showed how far he had moved in political ideology—and how far behind the French were in appreciating the degree of reform required. Next, in May of the same year, the Bey of Tunis angered the French. He presented a list of proposed reforms that would have greatly weakened the protectorate arrangement, by reasserting beylic autonomy. The French responded not with words, but with action. They deposed the Bey on charges of having collaborated with the Italian Fascists. Exile only enhanced the Bey's standing, as it also generated new enthusiasm for the Tunisian nationalist movement. Finally, in Morocco in December, the Istiqlal, or independence party, was founded—the outcome, in part, of a new mood that had developed since the Casablanca Conference in January. During that conference, President Roosevelt had met with the Sultan and had apparently expressed an interest in seeing Morocco independent after the war. Whatever his words, Roosevelt irritated the French by consulting the Sultan directly, and not through them.

During the war years, and most certainly in 1943, the Free French mounted two distinct campaigns: one that was clearly military and directed at the liberation of French national soil; and another, more political than military, that was directed at the protection of colonial soil from local liberation movements. Of course, the situation in Indochina was completely out of French hands until late in 1945. But in North Africa the Gaullists acted with a peremptoriness that seemed in keeping with the practices of earlier colonial governors: Monicef Bey of Tunisia was exiled, and so was the leader of the Moroccan Istiqlal Party, Ahmed Belafrej; and Abbas was placed under house arrest. At the same time, General De Gaulle responded to Abbas's Manifesto by introducing almost exactly the same reforms as had been put forward in the aborted Blum–Viollette bill of 1936.

Repression and reform were both part of the French response to indigenous demands for drastic change. As was clearly evident in their political behavior, the Gaullists had no more intention than their predecessors had had of allowing the empire to disintegrate. Nevertheless, General De Gaulle did no better than King Canute: he could not stem the tide of change. Between 1945 and 1954, events— particularly in Algeria and Indochina— moved so seriously against the French that the fate of the empire could no longer be in doubt.

Algeria, which before the war would not have been singled out as an area in turmoil, now erupted politically. In 1943, a new political party, named the Friends of the Manifesto and of Liberty (AML), was formed, almost immediately after the Manifesto had been issued. It not only unified the various opposition groups in a sort of coalition, but also won new support, so that by late in 1944 it claimed some 500,000 members. By 1945 Messali Hadj's political party was the dominant element in the AML, and, making even more severe demands of the French than Abbas had done, it in effect requested complete political severance. As disturbing as these developments were to the French, they paled before a major upheaval that took place during the week of May 8, following the Allied victory in Europe. Amidst the colonial rejoicing, Moslem groups took to the streets with banners and cries of independence. In the region of Constantine, enthusiasm and emotion flared up, with armed groups randomly killing European civilians. The French reaction to this outrage was marked: what amounted to a brief military campaign, complete with aerial bombings, was directed against the Moslem population. The casualty figures, never firmly fixed, were high, certainly running into the thousands. And along with this wanton destruction of life went the collapse of any hope of future colonial peace. The French novelist Albert Camus summed it up thus: "The French authorities imagined that this repression would end the rebellion. In fact, they gave the signal for its start." Even though public order was re-established, the Algerian nationalist movement continued to grow, as did the suspicions and anxieties of the French settler population. In theory assimilated to France, hence an integral part of the national territory, Algeria was on its way to becoming an alien armed camp.

The main zone of colonial stress was not yet in North Africa, however. It was Indochina. That area, which earlier had been considered the jewel of the French Empire, was now to be the catalyst that would speed up that empire's total dissolution.

Perhaps the most recognizable political feature of Indochina in 1945 was the absence of the French from any position of authority or military importance. While the French claimed the land as theirs once again, their claim was all but disregarded. With the war ending, the Allies determined that the northern region of Vietnam should be occupied by the Chinese Nationalists, who were greatly interested in doing so. The British occupied the southern region, but with a much smaller number of men. As for the French, they were treated callously by all. They found it exceptionally difficult to obtain transport or equipment; and their imprisoned compatriots were not released with any dispatch by the Allied occupying forces. The crowning calumny—certainly in French eyes—occurred when no French flag was displayed at the ceremonies marking the end of the Japanese occupation, although the Soviet flag was prominently flown and so was that of Ho's provisional government.

This incredible situation was the result of several factors. Not only were the military forces that the Gaullists could call on in this area few and ill equipped, but in addition the collapse of Japan found the Free French unprepared to return to Indochina. Equally important was the strong American attitude, expressed by President Roosevelt himself: French imperialism in Indochina was excoriated, and hence it was not desirable that the French should return. Finally, there were the quick and subtle moves undertaken by Ho Chi Minh to assert his authority. In August, before the Allied occupation, Ho had declared a "Provisional Government of the Democratic Republic of Vietnam," thus attempting to pre-empt any future French claims to sovereignty.

All the same, within a few months the impossible was turned into the tolerable, from the French point of view. The Americans ceased their military aid to Ho and never granted him the recognition that he so ardently desired. By the late fall the French had been able to mount an expeditionary force, equipped with American weapons acquired in Europe. Now Ho was in a position of perplexity: faced by both the French and the Chinese, each a threat to his independence movement. He chose the deal with the newer and more alien imperialists, the French. An agreement was signed on March 6, 1946, by which the French recognized the Republic of Vietnam and by which Ho agreed to incorporate that republic in an Indochinese Federation, to be part of the French Union.

The agreement was short-lived, as was inevitable, given the suspicion that each side felt and the political maneuvering that each side undertook to gain an advantage. What made the political situation so tentative and tense was the military one. Bernard Fall, the outstanding contemporary observer of the Vietnamese scene in the 1950s, assessed it thus in his book *Street Without Joy*: "The French forces sent to Indochina were too strong for France to resist the temptation of using them; yet not strong enough to keep the Viet Minh from trying to solve the whole political problem by throwing the French into the sea." The apparent military weakness of the other side emboldened the enemy to seek a military solution. And so, on December 17, 1946, after a series of military ambuscades in and around Hanoi, the Viet Minh began an all-out attack, which they declared to be a response to a previous French naval bombardment.

The subsequent history of Vietnam is military and tragic, with the French fighting a European-style war based on fixed lines and heavy equipment, while the Viet Minh engaged in guerrilla warfare, based on infiltration and lightly-armed small-scale military formations. For nearly eight years the French fought on, hoping to reach the victory that seemed constantly to elude them. The national economy was jeopardized; the military, which was determined to regain the luster it had lost in 1940, grew bitter and distrustful of the civilians; and the appalling example of battlefield indecisiveness had its effect on other colonial regions.

Finally, in a battle that should not have taken place, under circumstances that the careless but haughty French commanders could not appreciate, the military situation was dramatically turned in favor of the Viet Minh. Dien Bien Phu, a French outpost placed deep in Viet Minh territory in late 1953, found itself besieged in the spring of 1954. Although the French fought heroically, they were surrounded by Viet Minh artillery, which pounded the isolated fortress and made the one airstrip all but inaccessible to French supply. By May 7, 1954, the fortress was a tattered ruin, its defenders no longer able to hold on. With the fall of Dien Bien Phu went the fall of French Indochina. At the conference table in Geneva in October 1945, France finally and officially withdrew from Vietnam, leaving that wartorn country in a state of desolation, only to be made worse when the Americans later tried to succeed where the French had failed.

Dien Bien Phu can be seen as a dreadful modern version of the sort of heroic fortress-defense that had been a feature of the history of empire in the nineteenth century and had given the term *beau geste* a romantic ring; but its consequences were far more important. It was an awful signal that the French colonial empire was finished. On November 1, 1954, armed revolt broke out in Algeria. The second war of colonial devolution thereupon began, one that has been called the meanest, most vicious war in French history.

What made this second colonial war so intense, bitter and drawn-out—it did not end until 1962—was, principally, the general French desire not to repeat the mistakes made in Indochina. The French army, notably its paratroop batallions, which had fought so hard and at such cost in Indochina, thought that the worst lessons of that war had been well learned and could be effectively applied in Algeria. The government, for its part, was determined that the struggle should not fail for lack of men and equipment; and, whereas in Indochina the French forces had been composed entirely of volunteers, in Algeria they were swelled with conscripts. Then, of course, the civilian element, that large group called "settlers" whether they farmed or not, who numbered around 1 ½ million, had a deep stake in the war: they considered Algeria their homeland. All of these factors increased the national commitment, brought Algeria closer to France than it ever had been before, and, consequently, gave popular meaning to the familiar cry "Algeria is France."

The rebellion turned into a revolution, as many then and later wisely asserted. Initially, the National Liberation Front (FLN), which began the hostilities, had about 650 adherents. But, as the acts of terror escalated, so did the colonial repression, which served only to increase Algerian dissatisfaction and swell the support of the FLN. The moderates, of whom Ferhat Abbas had been one, disappeared (he joined the FLN). And French hopes to mediate the situation also disappeared, swept away by the wrath of the settlers, who now sought the repression of, not any compromise with, the revolutionary elements of the Arab population. The turning-point in the war occurred late in 1956, when the army was in effect given police powers and told to gain and maintain order. By then, Algeria had two governments, as described by Ferhat Abbas: a government of day, outwardly maintained by the French authorities; and a government of night, ruled severely and puritanically by the FLN. The liberation movement was now truly popular, rapidly increasing in membership and dominant in popular support.

As at the beginning under Marshal Bugeaud, Algeria again witnessed a form of military imperialism—not expansionist, now, but defensive. The most significant military action during this period was the "Battle of Algiers." Faced with what seemed a hopeless situation of intensifying assassination, amounting to some five or six deaths a day in Algiers, in February 1957 the government turned over police powers to the famous Tenth Paratroop Division, under the popular General Massu. One of the worst lessons learned in Indochina, the uses of torture, was now employed to learn of FLN activities and strongholds. The Battle of Algiers was won, and the FLN, its city leadership fragmented, took to the countryside, where the war dragged on.

However, the army's new authority, its political involvement in the affairs of Algeria, created a tense situation. Both military and settlers were growingly dissatisfied with what they considered to be vacillation and ineptness on the part of the government. The Fourth Republic, a weak series of coalition governments, suddenly found its very existence threatened. On May 13, 1958, a "Government of Public Safety" was thrown together in Algiers, its leadership given to

General Massu. Its essential demand was retention of French Algeria, but with integration for both the Moslem and French population. This political revolt against the authority of the Fourth Republic, coupled with fear of possible military action by the new rebels, led the President of the Republic to ask General De Gaulle to assume the Premiership. Within a month of the *treize mai* affair, the Fourth Republic was giving way to the Fifth. Once again, De Gaulle had to mediate the colonial affairs of France, but it was not until 1962 that an effective agreement was reached whereby the French withdrew from Algeria.

The struggles over Indochina and Algeria were no doubt the most violent episodes in the history of decolonization. The conflict over Algeria began as that over Indochina ended, so that together the two spanned the period during which the decolonization process was at its height. This in part explains the relative ease and good grace with which France departed from its other territories. Such a statement, however, is not designed to suggest that tension and violent interaction were not noticeable elsewhere. There were enough indications to the contrary. On March 29, 1947, a rebellion broke out in Madagascar that met with considerable initial success, but was subsequently suppressed by the French military. Tens of thousands of lives were lost, and hundreds of thousands were imprisoned. But the French and Malagasy were able to patch the surface of their political relations so that a general condition of peace reigned until independence in 1960. In Tunisia in March 1952, French troops, under orders of the new Resident, General Leclerc, began a "mopping up" operation in the area of Cape Bon, this designed to round up nationalists concentrated there. Although the loss of life was, fortunately, low, the many arrests and the generally brutal behavior of the French forces led to nationwide strikes and increasing nationalist opposition. By 1954 the French were seriously negotiating new terms with the Tunisian independence movement.

Terrible as such upheavals were, and evident as were the political uses of terror and murder on both sides, the decolonization of most of the French Empire followed not a military, but a diplomatic, pattern. In this regard the main developments were in Tunisia and Morocco. Despite the fact that the Bey of Tunis appeared as a mere cipher, while the Sultan of Morocco enjoyed the role of a national leader, Tunisia and Morocco followed a similar road to independence. As the nationalist movements grew in each country, so did the recalcitrance of the settlers. The home government, ever precarious in terms of its parliamentary support, attempted to negotiate, but did so primarily with the object of retaining for France as much authority as possible. Concepts such as internal sovereignty and interdependence were conjured up, out of resignation more than through inspiration. Complicating the general situation was the attitude of the local colonial administration, which often seemed more inclined to side with the "settlers" than to respond to metropolitan-French authority. At times the local French took independent, hasty action, as, for instance, on January 18, 1952, when Habib Bourguiba and some of his associates were arrested—without the metropolitan authorities' approval, or even knowledge.

When De Gaulle returned to power, Morocco and Tunisia had already gained their independence and Algeria was well on the way to achieving its own. This left the new President of the Fifth Republic the important task of reforming, before it, too, fell in disarray, the vast French colonial estate in Black Africa. However, the Community he proposed, which received such strong approval in the 1958 referendum, came into being only to disappear soon after.

Once Ghana, the former Gold Coast, had gained its independence (in 1957), the pattern of politics in sub-Saharan Africa took on a new cast. In 1958, Guinea, voting against the referendum, was given its independence with haughty displeasure. The departing French took everything with them, including the telephones. Yet Senghor, whose affinity for the French was well known, announced that he considered the referendum a move in the direction of independence. Thus, when the United Nations Trust Territories of Togo and Cameroon requested independence of French tutelage in 1960, this was granted and was an important precipitant of similar moves by neighboring states. The rest of the constituent members of the French Community became independent in the same year.

What remained of the French Empire after 1960 can only be described as vestigial: small bits of territory that would not add up to much in terms of French political power and that would not yield much in the way of raw materials to enhance the nation's economic condition. The swift disappearance of "French Africa" brought no traumatic results comparable to those which shook the country when the Algerian war of liberation intensified after 1956. Indeed, relations with most of the new black African states remained cordial, even warm. As President Senghor remarked, the real issue was to assimilate, not be assimilated, and so the influence of France remained— accepted not imposed, however.

In the greater scheme of world affairs, the reduction of France to nearly her own continental limits produced none of the dire effects that had been predicted from the 1950s on. It was then that the old myth of El Dorado was raised again, less to dazzle than to forewarn. The concept of Eurafrica, of a Franco-African economic community

bound together by mutual material interest, was posited. More particularly, critics spoke glowingly of the wealth of the Sahara. The
natural gas and oil hidden there would now be made available, thanks
to modern technology. In an article appearing in the July 1959 issue of
the American publication *Foreign Affairs*, Jacques Soustelle, former
High Commissioner in Algeria, explained the economic potential of
this area to unknowing American readers. And he concluded, "It is
not daydreaming to talk about these long-range plans.... We may
foresee that in years to come not only France but also a great part of
Europe will find in the Sahara the cheap power it so much needs for
rapid industrial growth."

There is no need to comment on the irony that has since intruded
into Soustelle's words. What is important is that no economic community, as earlier planned, developed. Nor, for that matter, did the
failure to realize it adversely affect France. As Raymond Aron, one of
France's most astute observers, remarked in his book *La Tragédie
algérienne* (1957), the Dutch withdrawal from the East Indies did not
cause their economy to plummet; indeed, continuation of the war in
Algeria would drain future resources, not guarantee present ones.

Aron was correct. The loss of empire coincided with the postwar
period of economic boom in France. The two were not closely related,
although the reduction of French military expenditures was an important factor. Perhaps the truth lies in what Germaine Tillion, in
L'Algérie en 1957, called "France's good luck and Algeria's bad."
France, with a handful of other nations, had found a secure place in the
modern industrial world. "That is why," she argued, "despite our
misfortunes and stupidities, we can still be called lucky, because, when
the fateful hour struck, we were to be found in the camp of the
winners."

The loss of empire was the loss of something that had always been
peripheral to French society and the general condition of the French
nation. If anywhere, empire had its most profound meaning—and
effect—away from France, in those many lands and among those
millions of peoples who were at one time subsumed under the name
France d'outre-mer.

Afterward

Within a short distance of the official residence of the President of the Republic of Senegal will be found a statue of Louis Faidherbe. The figure faces the sea, the eyes staring vacuously, as eyes of eminent figures should when fixed for what the sculptor hopes will be eternity. Faidherbe's statue has now outstayed his work, or that of any other Frenchman devoted to the old cause of empire.

This bronze emblem of empire nevertheless serves as a contemporary indication of the many effects of French expansion which still dot the countryside of lands formerly under the tricolor. Certain aspects of imperialism seem to have persisted where empire has crumbled. In fact, old and new French influences still mark off the previously colonial areas from their geographical neighbors. Most obvious is the difference in language, which even divides tribal groupings, as, for instance, the Wolof of Senegal and Gambia. The appearance of the tricolor as the most popular flag style in the nations of old French Africa says a little about the cultural effects of imperialism. And the choice of a French composer for the music of several of the new national anthems perhaps says a little more. The campaign for *francophonie* initially waged by President Senghor and now strongly centered in Montreal is an interesting development that speaks for itself. But imagine what a clever satirist, a modern Anatole France writing a modern *Île des Penguins*, might make of the *Club Méditerranée*, that lush and profit-making leisure-time institution, with its alabaster-white buildings occupying some of the finest beaches in the old empire—and in a manner that French marines could never have done.

None of these signs is in itself of great moment, but each does add some small evidence to the general assertion that decolonization more often than not meant modification, rather than total abolition, of the colonial system. Few were the areas at one time submitted to France that underwent the severe and puritanical change imposed by the Viet Minh. On the contrary, most pursued a policy of adaptation by negotiating treaties of assistance with the French and establishing amicable diplomatic relations. Even Algeria, the scene of such bitter strife, was soon thereafter willingly receiving French technicians and schoolteachers, with its national army equipped with French weapons of war. Moreover, a new form of colonization occurred which created new lines between former colonizer and colonized. Large numbers of Algerians and black Africans migrated to France. As perceived by many of these individuals, the new national state offered less economic opportunity than did the old colonial one. The Algerian migration became an important factor soon after World War II, but it intensified in the period of decolonization, as did the black–African. Just as the colonial city attracted persons from the countryside by its economic promise, so metropolitan France did in the waning years of colonialism.

In abstract cultural form, what is seen here is the continuing preponderance of an advanced technological order over a more rudimentary one. It is what Germaine Tillion put more simply and directly as "France's good luck." Early modernization has made France one of the world's few successful industrial nations. And, according to the American economist Eugene Staley, no nation outside the Western world, except Japan, has been able to achieve in the twentieth century what a few West European nations and the United States did in the nineteenth. That France is today the world's third major exporter of sophisticated military hardware is clear indication that the post-imperial age has in no way brought about the collapse of French influence and power.

In our age the world is meanly divided into two groups: the "rich nations" and the "poor nations." The English author Barbara Ward noted this in the early 1950s, and the condition, if it has changed, has done so for the worst. Dependence is an unfortunate characteristic of much of the former colonial world. And dependence breeds its own form of familiarity. The camshaft of a Berliot truck, for instance, cannot be readily supplied by an authorized General Motors or Bedford dealer. Even in this era of global interchangeability of parts, goods remain stamped by national culture as much as does language. Moreover, such dependency has in some instances increased. Since the colonial retreat, the French have poured large sums of money into aid. Military training, equipment, even troops have been supplied to many of the former French colonies of Black Africa. Subsidies to make products competitive in the market, as witness the French-supported

Senegalese peanut industry, have also tightened the economic bonds. Finally, after independence the banking network and the issue of currency continued to be controlled by French personnel and mechanisms—again, most clearly seen in the case of West Africa in the 1960s.

Many critics, particularly those given to a materialistic interpretation of history, have argued that "neo-colonialism" has replaced imperialism. This change consists in the wolf donning fox's clothing. Instead of military domination, with flags waving and bands playing, the operation is now quiet and quite subtle, manipulated by finance and the intricate forms of contemporary economic exchange, and directed toward the retention of a world of imbalance: rich, industrial nations exploiting poor, agricultural ones. According to this argument, the underlying purpose of imperialism has endured. The new nations have the façade and show of power; but the *éminence grise* is the capitalist, who is still able to satisfy his own interests. Critics supporting this line of reasoning have, in effect, brought Lenin up-to-date. Neo-colonialism is the last stage of imperialism. This epigram—also the title of a book by Kwame Nkrumah, the first President of Ghana—succinctly explains the new interpretation.

While this historical assessment of the continuing disparity in wealth between former colonizing power and former colonies has been a matter of lively, even acrimonious, academic debate, one social feature relating to economic modernization has been recognized with general consensus. Aimé Césaire put the matter this way in an article he wrote for *Présence africaine* in 1956: "What does history teach us about colonization? . . . That the technology of the colonizing country is always developed on the margin of the indigenous society and without the possibility ever being given to the colonized people to master it." Césaire, here in the company of a number of other critics, suggests that the impact of imperialism did not force Asia and Africa into modernity. Rather, by its very discriminatory nature, imperialism delayed the process, because the colonial population was selectively isolated from it.

The origins of this policy of social isolation are not difficult to find. They are late nineteenth century in date and paternalistic in mood. In French colonial practice, both the policy of "assimilation" and that of "association" were drawn from a familial assumption of responsibility and duty, with the colonizer as adult, the colonized as child. That image was frozen in the bronze statuary and concrete friezes with which the French adorned their public places in the colonial world. The image was also conveyed verbally. Albert Schweitzer, for instance, once remarked, "The negro is a child, and with children nothing can be done without the use of authority." Thoughts such as these led to practices in which a subordinate role was allocated to all but the most talented members of the indigenous population.

Interestingly, and perhaps expectedly, an important literature concerning the relationships between colonizer and colonized developed in the declining years of empire. To the older political and economic arguments were added new ones informed by modern research in sociology and psychology. Among the many authors who made contributions at this time, none has been accorded greater attention than the Tunisian Albert Memmi and the Martiniquan Frantz Fanon. Fanon has far outweighted Memmi in his general effect, but both offer insight into this complex problem of cultural and racial encounter.

Both critics assess colonialism as a form of debasement, creating conditions which deprive the colonized of his personality. For Memmi, in his *Portrait du colonisé*, published in 1957, both colonizer and colonized are fixed in roles they must play; one cannot exist without the other. Their relationship is situational. To justify his role of dominance, the colonizer must create an image of the colonized as weak, lazy, unreliable. "Thus, one after another, all the qualities which make a man crumble away," Memmi comments. In the new role assigned him, the colonized is "removed from history and the community." He is acted upon, an individual without judgment and responsibility.

Fanon was also greatly disturbed by this warped relationship, which he probed with poetic sensitivity and psychological insight in his *Peau noir, masques blancs*, first published in 1952. As the title eminently suggests, the black is forced to be false to himself, to assume a white mask. In asserting his feelings of superiority, the European has imposed a complementary feeling of inferiority upon the black. Therefore, the black anguish is bitterly endured in the attempt to escape from this condition. "Out of the blackest part of my soul, across the zebra striping of my mind, surges this desire to be suddenly *white*," Fanon cries in one of the most moving passages in the book. What he is proposing is that, by making life for the black an internalized, harrowing experience of self-doubt and socially-contrived damnation, the colonial situation has created a basic psycho–existential difficulty. Yet Fanon can offer no simple statement concerning what position ought be taken by those who have undergone what he has. He protests that he wishes to be an individual, not ensnared by a black past, nor imprisoned by a white, colonial present. There is, therefore, no conclusion to *Peau noir*. The author ends, rather, with the hope of a humanist deeply concerned with individuality. Fanon's revolutionary message appeared later, in his *Les Damnés de la terre* (1963), wherein the humanist has become the radical, now speaking of the therapeutic value of violence, the need to expunge the colonial act of forceful domination by its violent overthrow. No longer searching for individual catharsis, as he was in *Peau noir*, he now proposes that the way to national self-consciousness and collective dignity lies in the forceful struggle against colonialism.

While both Memmi and Fanon generalized about their own personal experiences—and Fanon added a number of case studies from his experience as a medical doctor in the service of the Algerian FLN—it is doubtful that the African in the bush or the Annamite in the rice paddy appreciated, in the way these two authors did, the disturbing ambiguity of the colonial situation. Fanon admitted as much when he stated that the peasant conceives of the revolutionary movement in terms of bread and land, not ideology and social theory. As members of the educated colonial elite, both authors witnessed and understood the inconsistencies within French colonial policy. In other words, they were sufficiently assimilated to know the nature of their own alienation from their particular culture, its people, and the land on which these were situated. Moreover, Memmi and Fanon wrote in French and addressed a European audience, not a colonial one. The fact that Jean-Paul Sartre provided an introduction for Memmi's book and a preface for Fanon's *Les Damnés* is proof of the influence of European thought on the structure and direction of these studies. "Europeans, you must open this book and enter into it," commands Sartre in his preface to Fanon's work.

In a peculiar way, the writing of Memmi and Fanon presents both a profound criticism of, and a great tribute to, French imperialism. These men belonged to that select group described in colonial literature as the *évolués*, those "natives" introduced to and allowed to participate in French civilization. They were, therefore, "assimilated" and were acutely conscious of the cultural ambiguity in which this involved them. But other *évolués*, more content and, perhaps, less observant, accepted their condition proudly. The social effects of French colonization are not easy to assess.

Broadly speaking, the French treated the mass of the colonial populations with indifference, occasionally with contempt, while they also willingly, even diligently, trained an elite. For a small number, therefore, assimilation was practised, and the idea of the universalism of French culture, with its Cartesian and 1789 Revolutionary individualism, was implanted in Martinique, Senegal, Madagascar and Indochina. There is dissent from this interpretation, however. In an extraordinarily interesting lecture that he offered as the Lugard Memorial Lecture of 1963, delivered in Brussels, and charmingly entitled "Et maintenant, Lord Lugard?", Hubert Deschamps argued that French imperialism was more democratic and integration- ist than elitist and isolationist. He contended that the introduction of French education at all levels in the school system in Africa helped avert a dichotomy between elite and mass. "Thus we have often avoided the divorce between the masses that remain traditional and the elite that have received a foreign education," he contended.

The point is that the cultural mission was and has remained the most important—and noble—in the minds of the practitioners and supporters of French empire. Moreover, Deschamps may be right in his further assertion, also made in the Lugard Memorial Lecture, that a sincere effort at political assimilation was undertaken in those years following World War II. He suggests that a new spirit of international federation animated the spirit of Frenchmen. Other critics, however, would contend that the spirit was one of desperation. Whichever, the French did belatedly try to create the social conditions that would allow for greater assimilation and thus make the old imperial ideal approximate to reality.

Now that the age of empire is over, the French have been far less defensive about the past—at least in print—than the British have. No one has written a book comparable, say, to Margery Perham's *The Colonial Reckoning*, or Sir Arthur Burns', *In Defence of Colonies*. Perhaps this is because the French Empire never figured in nation- al thought or purpose in quite the way that the British Empire did.

On the most obvious and colorful level, the ceremonial, the French could not mount the grand parades of empire that would suggest continuity, glory, and some sort of metaphysical union of national forces. Beginning with Victoria's two jubilees, the British provided a public ritual which has only gained in popularity. Against such theat- rical performance, the French have only offered the military parade down the Champs-Élysées on Bastille Day. True, the 1957 perfor- mance aroused applause and excitement, as the famous Third Regi- ment of Colonial Parachutists strode down the avenue, the contingent smartly arrayed in combat uniforms and its units led by the haughty form of Colonel Bigéard, then something of a national hero.

Yet even the heroism of empire was never so well contrived in France as across the Channel. For whatever reasons, the French had no G. A. Henty, no Rider Haggard, not even a Somerset Maugham, to blend into some appealing literary form that would inspire youth and distract adults the sorts of events that occurred and activities that were engaged in overseas. If anything, the French Empire was primarily the subject of essayists and moralists, particularly in the years of declining power, when the disintegrative effect of decolonization was widely lamented.

This lack of a literary genre of heroic colonial novels may well have been a corollary of the absence of a public-school tradition and, consequently, the atmosphere in which an imperial idea could grow to inspiring proportions. Several authors have said as much. Certainly the sense of aristocratic dedication that was admired and respected in Great Britain until the blunders committed on the battlefields of World War I never existed in France. Colonial personnel were seen in quite a different light. "It was said that only thick heads and dry fruit were sent overseas," remarked Hubert Deschamps in a discussion of the French Empire before 1914. Deschamps vigorously dissented from this opinion, but his conclusion does not alter the fact of the myth. The empire was not of heroic proportions in the eyes of most Frenchmen.

A further contributing factor to the differences between French and British appraisals of empire derives from the perceived relationship between nationalism and imperialism. By the end of the nineteenth century the two concepts were almost interchangeable in popular thought in Great Britain. And, certainly, the two great Durbars held in India, the first in honor of Edward VII in 1906, and the second attended by the new king, George V, in 1911, suggest a conscious effort to make of the king–emperor a unified political personage and hence to extend his spiritual and historical functions around the world. In France, there were two competing nationalisms, as Raoul Girardet has argued in his L'Idée coloniale en France (1972). First, there was the nationalism expressed by Georges Clemenceau and those who fixed their eyes on the Rhine. Continental in perspective, anti–German in direction, and revengeful in mood, this nationalism was fostered by individuals who considered overseas ventures national distractions. Juxtaposed with, occasionally in direct opposition to, these continental nationalists were the imperial nationalists, those who would rejuvenate France overseas. The latter group never won the public support that the former did, in part because empire was viewed as far away and exotic, not a vital condition of the nation's well-being. Jules Ferry once walked by a provocative dancer at a sideshow and commented to his companions that she represented what the empire meant to most Frenchmen.

Certainly it meant much more, but never enough to win over the hearts of a majority of the population or even a particular class within it. Seldom, therefore, was empire a major national issue. Tragically, the one occasion when the colonial situation did affect the nation profoundly was that of the Algerian war, which precipitated the fall of the Fourth Republic. By then the military had once again made imperialism their particular cause. And so, ironically, at the end as at the beginning, the army once more played a significant role in the affairs of empire.

Post-imperial France shows few marks—or scars—from the overseas past. Back in 1931, when the Parisian International Colonial Exposition was an event that allowed Hubert Lyautey to plan grandly for the future, a microcosmic empire was constructed in the Bois de Vincennes. Of the many buildings then put up, one was designed to be permanent: a colonial museum. The structure still greets the visitor standing before the gates to the Bois de Vincennes, although its name and functions have been expanded. What remains of the French Empire in the territories that formally constituted it is, of course, another history.

Booknotes

CHAPTER 1

It may seem somewhat surprising to learn that the second most significant of European colonial empires has not been the subject of a large number of historical analyses. This is all the more surprising in view of the fact that France is a nation which prides itself on the *grande synthèse historique*. To compound the problem further, the standard works in English which treat the French empire in its entirety were written before decolonization and are thus now outdated.

As Professor Henri Brunschwig has said, the French have not had the retrospective curiosity about their empire that the British have had about theirs. Yet such an argument is not meant to deny that there are many fine monographs, both in French and in English, dealing with major aspects of the French Empire (where, in the bibliographical notes that follow, reference is made to a work that has appeared in both French and English editions, details are given of the English edition only). The energetic reader can, therefore, find enough to satisfy his interests on nearly all aspects of the subject.

The most useful, modern introduction is that of Jean Ganiage, *L'Expansion coloniale de la France sous la Troisième République* (Paris, 1968). This is essentially a political history, but very balanced in its judgment and quite detailed. Stephen H. Roberts' *The History of French Colonial Policy, 1870–1925* (London, 1929), and Herbert I. Priestley's *France Overseas: A Study of Modern Imperialism* (New York, 1938) should be read with the caution that the events of the last thirty years require. Beyond these books are two newer general studies in which the French Empire is treated along with the empires of other European nations: David Fieldhouse, *The Colonial Empires From the Eighteenth Century* (London, 1966); and Raymond F. Betts, *The False Dawn: European Imperialism in the Nineteenth Century* (Minneapolis, 1975).

From a continental French perspective, the causal pattern of French imperialism has been well considered. The now-classic study on the subject is Henri Brunschwig, *French Colonialism, 1871–1914* (London, 1966), which stressed political causes and which first drew attention to the important role played by that pressure group known as the "colonial party." The initial work of Brunschwig has been greatly refined in an article the general reader will find both useful and fascinating: C. W. Andrew and A. S. Kanya-Forstner, "The French 'Colonial Party'; Its Composition, Aims and Influence, 1885–1914," *Historical Journal*, XIV (1971) 99–128. Among the most recent diplomatic studies, one in particular should be singled out: Christopher Andrew, *Théophile Delcassé and the Making of the Entente Cordiale: A Reappraisal of French Foreign Policy, 1898–1905* (London, 1968), in which the Moroccan question is given close analysis. As an interesting addition to this study of Delcassé, there is the article by Kim Munholland, "Rival Approaches to Morocco: Delcassé, Lyautey and the Algerian–Moroccan Border, 1903–1905," in *French Historical Studies*, V (1968) 328–43. The broader dimensions of French diplomacy are treated in René Albrecht-Carrié, *Britain and France: Adaptations to a Changing Context of Power* (New York, 1970).

There is growing academic interest in the role played by the French military in the establishment of colonial empire. A pace-setting work is A. S. Kanya-Forstner, *The Conquest of the Western Sudan: A Study in French Military Imperialism* (Cambridge, 1969), the general thesis of which has figured prominently in this chapter. In addition, Charles André Julien, *Histoire de l'Algérie contemporaine*, vol. I (Paris, 1964), provides a splendid introduction to the military activities of Bugeaud in Algeria. On French expansion in West Africa, where military men such as Faidherbe, Gallieni and Archimbaud were so active, the two studies by John Hargreaves are highly recommended: *Prelude to the Partition of West Africa* (London, 1963); and the first of its companion studies, *West Africa Partitioned*, vol. I, *The Loaded Pause* (Madison, Wis., 1974). For Lyautey's early activities in Morocco, see General Georges Catroux, *Lyautey le marocain* (Paris, 1952).

The role of the navy, particularly in Indochina, where its activities mingled with those of the missionaries, is told in a fine analysis by John F. Cady, *The Roots of French Imperialism in Eastern Asia* (Ithaca, NY, 1967). The treatment of this subject in the present chapter relies very heavily on Cady's interpretation. Finally, mention should be made of Henri Brunschwig, "Anglophobia and French African Policy," in Prosser Gifford and William Roger Louis (eds), *France and Britain in Africa* (New Haven, Conn., 1971), wherein naval policy is also considered.

The subject of the economic roots of imperial expansion has not generated the same sort of controversy in France as it has in Great Britain. But there are a few prominent studies that suggest new historical considerations opposing the more traditional nationalist argument. Among the most recent works whose interpretations have affected this chapter, as well as most historical thinking on the subject, are David Landes, *Bankers and Pashas, International Finance and Economic Imperialism in Egypt* (Cambridge, Mass., 1958); Jean Ganiage, *Les Origines du protectorat français en Tunisie, 1861–1881* (Paris, 1959), which, like the Landes volume, is excellent on the role of international finance; Pierre Guillen, "L'Implantation de Schneider au Maroc—Les débuts de la Compagnie marocaine (1902–1906)", *Revue d'histoire diplomatique*, LXXIX (1965) 113–68; and John F. Laffey, "Roots of French Imperialism in the Nineteenth Century: The Case of Lyon," *French Historical Studies*, VI (1969) 78–92.

On particular "hotspots" of empire, a rich literature exists and allows the reader to discern how complicated the interplay of European diplomacy and local colonial activity often was. Perhaps the finest study of all is G. N. Sanderson, *England, Europe, and the Upper Nile, 1892–1899* (Edinburgh, 1965), which is now the standard work on events leading to Fashoda. On West Africa, the two volumes written by John D. Hargreaves, cited above, are of major importance. To these should be added the widely-acclaimed study by Bernard Schnapper, *La Politique et la commerce français dans le Golfe de Guinée de 1838 à 1871* (Paris, 1961). Also worth reading with care is Colin Newbury's article "The Development of French Policy on the Lower and Upper Niger, 1880–1898," *Journal of Modern History*, XXXI (1959) 16–26. One of the most recent revisionist articles, which centers the cause of the "Scramble" back in the Parisian ministries, is Colin W. Newbury and A. S. Kanya-Forstner, "French Policy and the Origins of the Scramble for West Africa," *Journal of African History*, X (1969) 253–76. On French penetration into Indochina, see Milton E. Osborne, *The French Presence in Cochinchina and Cambodia: Rule and Response, 1885–1905* (Ithaca, NY, 1969). And also consult the fine studies by Edmund Burke III, *Prelude to Protectorate in Morocco: Precolonial Protest and Resistance, 1860–1912* (Chicago, 1976), which keeps a nice balance between French intentions and Moroccan resistance; and that of Russ E. Dunn, Resistance In the Desert: Moroccan Response to Imperialism, 1881–1912 (Madison, Wis., 1977).

CHAPTER 2

In recent years French theories of imperialism have attracted more scholarly attention than before. However, the range of thought and the depth of economic analysis found in theories elaborated in Great Britain and Germany were not characteristics of French imperialist ideology and, perhaps, explain the still-small number of historical interpretations by French writers.

The one study that presents an excellent survey of ideological development from the outset of the "New Imperialism" until the demise of empire is Raoul Girardet, *L'Idée coloniale en France de 1871 à 1962* (Paris, 1972). Weaving political speeches, academic treatises, and colonial fiction together with a most commendable skill, Girardet describes how French colonial ideas, essentially united in the thought of Jules Ferry, made their way through modern French politics. Anyone interested in comparative colonial history would do well to read this volume in conjunction with A. P. Thornton's *Imperial Idea and Its Enemies: A Study in Power* (1959), to see how the British and French compared in the way they handled their imperial metaphysics.

For the early development of imperialist thought in France, there is the reliable, if somewhat cautious, interpretation by Agnes Murphy, *The Ideology of French Imperialism, 1871–1881* (Washington, DC, 1948), to which might be added the article by Donald McKay, "Colonialism in the French Geographical Movement, 1871–1881," *Geographical Review*, XXXIII (1943) 214–32. Following the Murphy volume chronologically, but concentrating on the ideological debate over colonial policy, is Raymond F. Betts, *Assimilation and Association in French Colonial Theory, 1890–1914* (New York, 1961). On the same subject, but broader in its chronological treatment is the article by M. D. Lewis, "One Million Frenchmen: The Assimilation Theory in

French Colonial Policy," *Comparative Studies in Society and History*, IV (1962) 129–53.

A number of biographies concerning the major proponents of empire and their arguments are readily available. The most significant are Thomas F. Power, *Jules Ferry and the Renaissance of French Imperialism* (New York, 1946); and Fresnette Ferry-Pisani, *Jules Ferry et le partage du monde* (Paris, 1962). A more popularly-turned work is Maurice Reclus, *Jules Ferry* (Paris, 1946). On Étienne there is the good study by H. Sieberg, *Eugène Étienne und die franzözische Kolonialpolitik, 1887–1904* (Cologne, 1968). As for the polemical activities of Joseph Chailley-Bert, see S. M. Persell, "Joseph Chailley-Bert and the Importance of the Union coloniale francaise," *Historical Journal*, XVII (1974) 176–84.

Concerning the development of a colonial mood in the fictional literature of the period, the most accessible work is Suzanne Howe, *Novels of Empire* (New York, 1949), a book whose obvious virtue is the catalogue of authors and works it provides. On French literature the standard work is Roland Lebel, *Histoire de la littérature coloniale* (Paris, 1931). However, there is a splendid recent study that provides a fascinating appraisal of the images conjured up from the colonial situation: Martine Astier Loutfi, *Littérature et colonialisme* (Paris, 1971).

An attempt to situate colonial thought and activity in a frontier setting is made in Raymond F. Betts, "The French Colonial Frontier," in Charles A. Warner (ed.), *From the Ancien Regime to the Popular Front* (New York, 1969).

CHAPTER 3

The French colonial officers, certainly the outstanding ones, committed themselves to authorship with almost as much diligence as to colonial affairs. Consequently, the historian has an abundance of material to review on the process of military conquest and "pacification," as seen from the various perspectives of the men who undertook it.

Among the major works available are General Paul Azan (ed.), *Par l'épee et par la charrue: écrits et discours de Bugeaud* (Paris, 1948)—from which most of the quotations in this chapter come; Louis Faidherbe, *Le Sénégal: la France dans l'Afrique occidentale* (Paris, 1889); Joseph Gallieni, *Gallieni au Tonkin, 1882–1896* (Paris, 1941), and *Neuf ans à Madagascar* (Paris, 1908)—an invaluable source heavily used here; and Hubert Lyautey, *Lettres de Tonkin et de Madagascar* (Paris, 1903), and—the most important of his works—*Paroles d'action* (Paris, 1927).

There are also many biographies available. See the sympathetic treatment afforded Faidherbe in Georges Hardy, *Faidherbe* (Paris, 1947). More critical is Leland C. Barrow's article "The Merchants and General Faidherbe: Aspects of French Expansion in Senegal in the 1850s," *Revue française d'histoire d'outre-mer* LXI (1974) 236–83. On Gallieni, there is Hubert Deschamps (ed.), *Gallieni pacificateur* (Paris, 1949), a good collection of Gallieni's writings, with a critical introduction by Deschamps. Much more useful, because more detailed, is Pierre Lyautey, *Gallieni* (Paris, 1959).

The greatest collection of biographies centers on Lyautey, whose posing, a bit like that of Puccini, his contemporary, made him an attractive figure.

Sonia E. Howe's *Lyautey of Morocco—An Authorized Life* (London, 1931) is a mellow study, a fitting ornament for Lyautey, then in his old age and highly respected. André Maurois's *Lyautey* (Paris, 1931) is a very favorable biography, written with the skill and verve for which Maurois was well known. *Lyautey le marocain* (Paris, 1952), by General Georges Catroux, is good for the early era of the Moroccan occupation. And Alam Scham's *Lyautey in Morocco: Protectorate Administration, 1912–1925* (Berkeley, Calif., 1970) is a good institutional study.

Treatment of French colonial policy has usually been critical, with the French emerging poorly in any general comparison between French and British African policies. As the issue of "indirect rule" was one of major concern in both countries after World War I, and as comparisons were then made on both sides, it seems fitting that retrospective analysis should follow a comparative approach. Hubert Deschamps, "Et maintenant, Lord Lugard?", *Africa*, XXXIII (1963) 293–305, is a delightful lecture, designed to suggest that in procedure and accomplishments the French and British were more alike than not. In direct reply is Michael Crowder's important article "Indirect Rule—French and British Style," *Africa*, XXXIV (1964) 197–205, in which the author demonstrates that, whereas usually, under the French system, the role of the local chief was largely subsumed under that of the French colonial officer, thus making indigenous government a part of French bureaucracy, the British method was to associate with the local chief in an advisory capacity. In part a test of this theory, A. I. Asiwaju, *Western Yorubaland Under European Rule, 1889–1945* (Atlantic Highlands, NJ, 1976), shows how greater flexibility and consideration on the part of the British led to better relations between conquered and conqueror than did French policy.

One particular study of French policy should be singled out: it is Charles-Robert Ageron's magisterial work on Algeria, *Les Algériens musulmans et la France, 1871–1919*, 2 vols (Paris, 1968), an extraordinarily detailed and fine analysis of the different institutions affected by French rule.

Among the other studies worth considering are Robert Bidwell, *Morocco Under Colonial Rule: French Administration of Tribal Areas, 1912–1956* (London, 1973); and Henri Brunschwig, "French Colonization, Exploration and Conquest in Tropical Africa from 1865 to 1898," in L. H. Gann and Peter Duignan (eds), *Colonialism in Africa*, vol. I of *The History and Politics of Colonialism, 1870–1914* (Cambridge, 1969).

CHAPTER 4

In terms of the studies they have generated, the structure and institutions of French colonial empire have been among the most popular aspects of it. Even as the empire was being put together, works concerned with railroad-building policy (then a favorite French dissertation topic), tariff policy, and aspects of colonial legislation were making their appearance. The many-times-reprinted standard work by Arthur Girault, *Principes de colonisation et de législation coloniale* (Paris, 1895), made its debut before Lyautey had made his in Morocco. This study grew in size, from reprinting to reprinting, until in 1930 it consisted of five volumes. It still remains a valuable source on its topic.

Just about the time Girault's work reached its final revision, a young American scholar took an active interest in French colonial organization. Virginia Thompson is one of those unusual figures to whom every historian of French colonial empire owes a great debt. Her meticulous and far-ranging scholarship has resulted in an encyclopedia of information, much of which has been used in this book. With her husband, Richard Adloff, she has continued her work until the present. Beginning with *French Indochina* (New York, 1937), her studies have covered a large number of French colonial territories. Adloff and Thompson have written the following: *French West Africa* (Stanford, Calif., 1957); *French Equatorial Africa* (Stanford, Calif., 1960); *The Malagasy Republic Today* (Stanford, Calif., 1965); *Djibouti and the Horn of Africa* (Stanford, Calif., 1968); and, most recently, *The French Pacific Islands* (Berkeley, Calif., 1971). Each volume contains an institutional survey, both descriptive and analytical, preceded by a historical introduction.

On the *mise en valeur* of the empire, the basic work is, course, Albert Sarraut, *La Mise en valeur des colonies françaises* (Paris, 1923), which is not only polemical but also a valuable statistical survey. The favorable interpretation provided by Sarraut may be offset by the severe interpretation provided by Jean Suret-Canale, *French Colonialism in Tropical Africa, 1900–1945* (New York, 1971). This work by an author of leftist persuasion offers a great deal of evidence to support the argument that French labor policy was exploitative and frequently inhumane. Anyone wishing to explore the problems with the concession companies should read Suret-Canale carefully. Concerned with the same subject is Catherine Coquery-Vidrovitch, "Quelques problèmes posés par le choix économique des grandes compagnies concessionnaires au Congo français, 1900–1920," *Bulletin de la Société d'Histoire Moderne*, I (1968) 2–13.

For North Africa and the effects of French development policy there, the reader would do well to turn to Jacques Berque's critical and intelligent analysis *French North Africa: The Maghrib Between Two World Wars* (London, 1967). The more detailed and historically organized study by Roger Le Tourneau, *L'Évolution politique de l'Afrique du Nord musulmane, 1920–1961* (Paris, 1962), is also worth consulting.

On particular institutions, there are several studies that bear consideration in a general survey. First is William B. Cohen's careful assessment of the French colonial service, *Rulers of Empire: The French Colonial Service in Africa* (Stanford, Calif., 1971), which contains an excellent analysis of the role of the École Coloniale and its personnel. The Force Noire is a subject that only recently has been given careful historical attention. The best introduction to the subject is Myron J. Echenberg, "Playing the Blood Tax: Military Conscription in French West Africa, 1914–1929," *Centre for Developing Area Studies*, Reprint Series, no. 40 (Montreal, 1976). An excellent statistical study is that by Marc Michel, "Le Recrutement des tirailleurs en A. O. F. pendant la première Guerre mondiale," *Revue française d'histoire d'outre-mer*, LX (1973) 644–60. And finally, the interested reader might look at Abdoulaye Ly, *Mercenaires noirs* (Paris, 1957), an indictment by an African.

On educational policy, there is no single work of an empire-wide synthesis. For Indochina, see the relevant chapters in Milton E. Osborne, *The French Presence in Cochinchina and Cambodia* (Ithaca, NY, 1969). A severe criticism of French educational intentions in Vietnam is Gail P. Kelly, "Colonial Schools in Vietnam, 1918 to 1938," *Proceedings of the Second Annual Meeting of the French Colonial Historical Society* (1977). On Black Africa, see Denise Bouche's "Les Écoles françaises au Soudan à l'époque de la conquête, 1884–1900," *Cahiers d'études africaines*, VI (1966) 288–97. Also of use is Prosser Gifford and Timothy C. Weiskel, "African Education in a Colonial Context: French and British Styles," in Prosser Gifford and William Roger Louis (eds), *France and Britain in Africa* (New Haven, Conn., 1971). The best general survey is Helen Kitchen (ed.), *The Educated African: A Country-By Country Survey of Educational Development in Africa* (New York, 1962).

The technology of French imperialism has not yet received the critical historical attention it merits. Some years ago Henri Brunschwig provided, as he often has, a pace-setting article, "Notes sur les technocrats de l'impérialisme française en Afrique noire," *Revue française d'histoire d'outre-mer*, LIV (1957) 171–87. The article was an attempt to show how imperialism was shaped by the schemes and dreams of engineers. Since then, several American doctoral dissertations have concentrated on the general subject, with Paul Pheffer using his dissertation as the basis for an article entitled "Political and Economic Strategies for French Colonial Railroads in West Africa—The Senegal–Sudan Rail Axis," in *Proceedings of the Second Annual Meeting of the French Colonial Historical Society* (1976). There is also an interesting account of early automobile use in West Africa: Yves J. St Martin, "Les Premières automobiles sur les bords du Niger," *Revue française d'histoire d'outre-mer*, LX (1973) 589–615.

Throughout this chapter the influence of Robert Delavignette has been marked. Certainly his little volume *Freedom and Authority in West Africa* (London, 1950), the English translation of *Service africain*, would occupy a prominent position in any bibliography on the structure and institutions of the French Empire.

CHAPTER 5

Although urban history in the "third world" has generated much enthusiasm among social scientists, particularly urban sociologists, it has not been studied in chronological depth. Most studies are concerned with the city as the focal point of modernization, and therefore research has concentrated on the social setting, with its problems of self–identification and unemployment. Books on French colonial urban development have consequently been few, and, though the French are now expressing new scholarly interest in the subject, no overall treatment of colonial urbanization is currently available. The present author is, however, working on such a project, and most of the material that appears in this particular chapter derives from his own research.

The best brief introduction to the study of urbanization in the colonial world is Gerald Breese, *Urbanization in Newly Developing Countries* (Englewood Cliffs, NJ, 1966). A structural analysis, this little book provides a good assessment of the general problems arising from recent urbanization in Asia, Latin America, and Africa, and from it valuable information relating to the French colonial experience can be extrapolated. Of a similar sort is the series of essays edited by Thomas Miner, *The City in Modern Africa* (New York, 1967). For a general analysis of the Asian setting, turn to T. G. McGee,

The Southeast Asian City (New York, 1967). More important for an understanding of the multiple roles played by the colonial city, as a third-world
metropolis, is Assane Seck, "Introduction à l'étude des villes tropicales,"
Tiers-Monde, VI (1965) 171–204.

On particular French colonial cities, there are several good work. The best
is without question André Adam's *Casablanca, essai sur la transformation de la
société marocaine au contact de l'Occident* (Paris, 1968). Somewhat polemical but
excellent in its criticism of urban planning by colonial authorities is *Casablanca* (Paris, 1955) by Michel Ecochard, a well-known urbanist. On the
arrival of a European "colony" in Casablanca, refer to Jean-Louis Miège and
Eugénie Hugues, *Les Européens á Casablanca au XIXᵉ siècle (1856–1906)*
(Paris, 1954). For the other main Europeanized city in French North Africa,
see the older but well-prepared study by René Lespès, *Alger, étude de géog-
raphie et d'histoire urbaine* (Paris, 1930).

On West African urban development there is a nice little body of literature, the most significant element of which is Assane Seck's splendid study
Dakar, métropole ouest-africaine (Dakar, 1970). Primarily concerned with
urban development in the recent past and in the first years of national
independence, this study is topical, not historical, but a remarkable example
of urban geography and sociology. Several brief monographs offer a suitable
historical introduction to Seck's work. There are the well-wrought article by
Roger Pasquier, "Villes du Sénégal au XIXᵉ siècle," *Revue française d'histoire
d'outre-mer*, XLVII (1960) 387–426, and the social interpretation by Jacques
Dresch, "Villes de l'Afrique occidentale," *Cahiers d'outre-mer*, XI (1960)
200–30. For a more recent observation of the economic importance of Dakar,
see Richard J. Peterec, *Dakar and West African Economic Development* (New
York, 1967).

Within any listing of major studies on African urban history, two books
would figure prominently. The first is a pace-setting interpretation, recognized for the quality of its field research: Horace Miner, *The Primitive City of
Timbuctoo* (Princeton, NJ, 1953). This study, the main part of the research for
which was undertaken in 1940, offers important insights into the colonial
situation of the time. The other work is of a broader canvas, and hence is an
excellent background to social change in an African urban setting: Georges
Balandier, *Sociologie des Brazzavilles noires* (1955), which has been translated
into English as *The Sociology of Black Africa* (London, 1970).

CHAPTER 6

The literature available on colonial protest movements is almost as great as
the literature of protest itself. Indeed, the subject has a particular intellectual
fascination, because it suggests both a cultural and an ideological awakening,
one that has impressively marked the modern era. Richly recorded in poetry,
fiction, political tracts, and journals of opinion, colonial protest has been
followed by the intellectual historian concerned with the translation of European thought into a new social environment, and by the social scientist
seeking to construct models of social behavior in the process of "modernization."

Perhaps the most popular of the historical subjects is that of the emergence
of a new cultural consciousness among black Africans. The basic work is that

of the Belgian author Lilyan Kesteloot, *Les Écrivains noirs de langue française: naissance d'une littérature* (Brussels, 1963). Of particular value to an understanding of the cultural developments in interwar Paris, the book is enriched from the correspondence that Kesteloot has had with many of the prominent figures of the time. A broader survey and an excellent reference work is Janheinz Jahn, *Neo-African Literature: A History of Black Writing* (New York, 1968). Geographically more restricted, but comparing protest in French with protest in British colonies, is Robert W. July, *The Origins of Modern African Thought* (New York, 1967), a splendid analytical survey of the major trends in nineteenth and twentieth century West African thought. George Shepperson's "Notes on Negro-American Influences on the Emergence of African Nationalism," in *Journal of African History*, I (1960) 299–312, is a good brief assessment of these intellectual developments. Particular biographies worth consulting are two on Senghor: Irving L. Markowitz, *Léopold Sédar Senghor and the Politics of Negritude* (New York, 1969); and Jacques Hymans, *Léopold Sédar Senghor: An Intellectual Biography* (Edinburgh, 1971).

Next in significance is the literary and political protest movement in Indochina. Several fine studies have recently been published, allowing the general reader the opportunity to survey the complex and intensifying mood of opposition in interwar Indochina. David G. Marr, *Vietnamese Anticolonialism, 1885–1925* (Berkeley, Calif., 1971), is a fine revision of a doctoral dissertation, and particularly useful as a guide to early protest, here demonstrated to be coincidental with the advent of French rule. A companion piece, less original in research and approach, but a good general survey, is William J. Duiker, *The Rise of Vietnamese Nationalism, 1900–1941* (Ithaca, NY, 1976). More detailed and very readable is Joseph Buttinger, *Viet-Nam: A Dragon Embattled*, 2 vols (New York, 1967). For a brief attempt at historical definition of the phrases of nationalist development in Indochina, see Jean Chesneaux, "Stages in the Development of the Vietnam National Movement," *Past and Present*, VII (1955) 63–75. Above all, the biography of Nguyen Ai Quoc by Jean Lacouture is recommended: *Ho Chi Minh* (New York, 1968).

The North African political scene can be approached through several good syntheses. Again, Jacques Berque's *North Africa: The Maghrib Between Two World Wars* (London, 1967), is worth reading in this historical context. So also is Charles André Julien's *L'Afrique du Nord en marche: nationalismes musulmanes et souveraineté française* (Paris, 1952). On Moroccan nationalist development, see John P. Halstead, *Rebirth of a Nation: The Origins and Rise of Moroccan Nationalism, 1912–1914* (Cambridge, 1967). On Tunisia, there is a nice little synthesis by Dwight Ling, *Tunisia: From Protectorate to Republic* (Bloomington, Ind., 1967). Félix Garras, *Bourguiba et la naissance d'une nation* (Paris, 1956), lives up to its title and will allow the reader to measure the extent of Bourguiba's role in national liberation. More theoretical is Charles A. Micaud (ed.), *Tunisia: The Politics of Modernization* (New York, 1964), the first part of which, "Stages in the Process of Change," by Leon Carl Brown, is an attempt to provide a historical model. Also of major importance, but not so readily accessible, is Nicola A. Ziadeh, *Origins of Nationalism in Tunisia* (Beirut, 1962). Nigel Heseltine's slim volume *Madagascar* (London, 1971) offers a good, brief introduction to Malagasy protest movements. On the same subject see Hubert Deschamps, *Histoire de Madagascar* (Paris, 1960). On the situation in Senegal, see G. Wesley Johnson, Jr, *The Emergence of Black Politics in Senegal* (Stanford, Calif., 1971), excellent on interwar developments and the role played by Blaise Diagne.

CHAPTER 7

No subject in any nation's modern colonial history has received wider and more detailed consideration than that generally termed "decolonization." The reasons are obvious: not only was the process of worldwide significance, but, in addition, it unfolded at the time when social-science techniques—models, systems analysis, role-playing, cultural contact—had reached a high degree of sophistication. Put otherwise, "decolonization" offered a particular opportunity to "test" new concepts—and, perhaps, to generate them.

The chronological emphasis of such studies is, therefore, on the post-World War devolution of the French colonial empire. There are, unfortunately, too few good reviews of developments during the war period itself. Vichy is only just coming into its own as a worthy historical topic, but the general reader can feel reasonably hopeful that the colonial aspects of the Vichy period will soon be brought into good historical light. Among the most valuable works for the period are General De Gaulle's *War Memoirs*, 3 vols (London, 1955–9), generally acknowledged as the best by any wartime leader. General F. J. Ingold, *La France et son empire dans la guerre* (Paris, 1946), supports the De Gaulle interpretation with its examination of the role of the French. Moreover, Brian Weinstein's splendid biography *Eboué* (New York, 1972) provides a good assessment of the Brazzaville Conference. The research of Dorothy Shipley White merits particular attention. Her "De Gaulle and the Decolonization of Black Africa," in *Proceedings of the French Colonial Historical Society* (1976), is a preface to a larger study now being prepared for publication.

Among the many general works dealing with decolonization, Rudolph von Albertini's *Decolonization* (New York, 1971), which includes a detailed and sensitive treatment of the French experience, is exceptional. Henri Grimal's *La Décolonisation, 1919–1963* (Paris, 1966) offers a good survey. More philosophical and provocative is Jacques Berque, *Dépossession du monde* (Paris, 1964), which ranges over a variety of subjects relating to imperialism and contains an interesting chapter entitled "Les Valeurs de la décolonisation." On a more specific subject, but of major importance to an understanding of France's position, is the recent work of Paul C. Sorum, *Intellectuals and Decolonization in France* (Chapel Hill, North Carolina, 1977).

A number of good studies exist on the French decolonizing experience in Black Africa. Broad treatment of French African policy is offered in Edward Mortimer, *France and the Africans, 1944–1960* (London, 1969). An excellent thematic study is that by D. Bruce Marshall, *The French Colonial Myth and Constitution Making in the Fourth Republic* (New Haven, Conn., 1971). The effort to establish the French Union, and the attitude of the black African leaders to this endeavor are subjects very well treated in this book. For the emergence of political parties in Black Africa, see Ruth Schachter Morgenthau, *Political Parties in French-Speaking West Africa*, (New York, 1964), which complements Marshall's work.

Vietnam, as a compounded tragedy involving first the French and then the Americans, has been a subject deeply probed. The most significant and powerful studies are those by Bernard Fall. His *Street Without Joy* (New York, 1964) and *The Two Vietnams* (London, 1964) will be read with great profit. Jean Lacouture's *Vietnam entre deux paix* (Paris, 1965) is a very good account of the tortuous process of decolonization, and his *Ho Chi Minh* (New York, 1968) is, of course, most useful for this period. Paul Mus's *Viet-nam, sociologie d'une guerre* (Paris, 1952) has a peculiar value, for it was written at a time when the outcome of the war was yet undetermined. Mus, a very sensitive Frenchman, desperately urged reform.

Even more painful in its effect on France was the concluding drama in Algeria. Because this war shook the foundations of the French nation and precipitated the fall of the Fourth Republic, it was found a compelling subject by large numbers of historians and journalists. David Gordon, in *The Passing of French Algeria* (London, 1966), paints on a large canvas, tracing the movement for liberation from the interwar period until the departure of the French. His book is well organized and written. *Algeria and France: From Colonialism to Cooperation* (London, 1963) is a brief study by Dorothy Pickles, English political scientist and a frequent author on French affairs. It provides a good introduction for the general reader, and places particular emphasis on the effects of the colonial war on metropolitan France. Jules Roy's *The War in Algeria* (London, 1961) and Jean-Jacques Servan-Schreiber's *Lieutenant in Algeria* (New York, 1957) are two contemporary accounts, both by journalists and both written from a personal perspective; they are engaging studies. The detailed development of the Algerian resistance movements is presented with clarity and conciseness in Alf Andrew Heggoy, *Insurgency and Counter-Insurgency in Algeria* (Bloomington, Ind., 1972). Finally, Germaine Tillion's *France and Algeria, Complementary Enemies* (New York, 1961) is one of those perceptive little volumes that rank the French among the world's best essayists of *moeurs*.

Less traumatic, the experience of France's other two North African possessions has aroused less intellectual concern. On Morocco in its period of transition from protectorate to independence is the splendid analysis by Jean and Simone Lacouture, *Le Maroc à l'épreuve* (Paris, 1968). Also, consult Douglas Ashford, *Political Change in Morocco* (Princeton, NJ, 1961), which contains useful background information on the independence movement. On Tunisia, see again Ling's *Tunisia: From Protectorate to Republic* (Bloomington, Ind., 1967).

On the final efforts of the French to restructure the old empire, there is quite a abundant literature in French. As already mentioned, Bruce D. Marshall's *The French Colonial Myth* offers an excellent assessment of the debate over the French Union. Similarly, Paul Mus's *Le Destin de l'Union française: De l'Indochine à l'Afrique* (Paris, 1954) is the appeal of an intelligent critic. On the French Community, perhaps the most handy volume is Yves Guena, *Historique de la Communauté* (Paris, 1962). Also see Jean Ehrhard's *Communauté ou Sécession* (Paris, 1959), a more journalistic account.

Index

The user is invited to consult the entry 'Colonial Empire' which will give a lead to the various aspects of government and social conditions general to 'France Overseas'; and to the entry for the individual city or country for matters exclusive to them. In respect of national aspirations (which is dealt with under the word 'Native') the reader should also consult the names of individual people. The letter-by-letter system of alphabetization has been adopted.

Abbas, Ferhat, 117, 119, 128, 131, 142, 146
Abd-el-Kader, 57, 59
Abidjan, 112
Administration, oversea, see Development of Colonies
Ahmadou Omar, 24
Ahmadou Segou, 62
Air travel, 94–5
Alexandria, British attack on (1882), 32
Algeria:
    expeditionary forces in (1830), 20
    Farmer settlers of, 79, 112
    FLN, 146
    military control of, 55–60
    1942 invasion of, 135
    post-Independence links with France, 151, 156–7
    resistance movement, 139, 143, 145–9
    see also Abbas, Ferhat; Hadj, Messali
Algiers, 98, 108–11, 146–7
Alsace and Lorraine controversy, 18, 98
AML Movement, 143
Anfreville de Salle, Dr, 114
Angkor Thom, 98
Annam, 25–7, 69–70, 130, 135
    see also Indochina; Ho Chi Minh
Antonetti, Raphaël-Valentin-Mauris, 83, 89–90
Arab Bureaux (in Algeria), 58–9
Arabi, Colonel, 31–2
Archinard, Colonel Louis, 24
Architecture, 101–2, 104, 106
Aron, Raymond, 149
Association policy, 49, 51 67–8, 73, 86, 89, 152
Atlantic, French islands in, 19

Baker, Josephine, 122
Balzac, Honoré de, 41
Bao Dai, 136

Barrès, Maurice, 39
Belafrej, Ahmed, 142
Bérard, Victor, 30
Berque, Jacques, 120
Bert, Paul, 70, 133
Bigéard, Colonel, 155
Bismarck, Prince Otto von, 18
Blum, Léon, 119–20, 130
Boilat, Abbé, 85–6
Bonard, Adm. Louis-Adolphe, 69
Bône, 98
Borgnis-Desbordes, Colonel, 24
Bouet-Willaumez, Mons., 85
Bourget, Paul, 41
Bourguiba, Habib, 121, 128, 129, 131, 148
Brazzaville, 112, 134, 136, 137
Bréton, André, 123
Brunschwig, Henri, 14
Buell, Raymond Leslie, 84
Bugeaud, Marshal Thomas, 23, 24, 55–60, 67

Cambon, Paul, 71
Cameroon, 35, 134, 148
Camus, Albert, 143
Canard, Louis, 77, 82
Can Vuong Movement, 130
Capital investment, 75–6, 78–9, 151–2
Cars, advent of, 93–4
Casablanca, 29, 67, 135
Cendrars, Blaise, 122
Césaire, Aimé, 121, 123–4, 152
Chailley-Bert, Joseph, 34, 37, 41, 47, 49, 52–3, 75
Cherifian Government, 67, 71
Ch'i-ch'ao, 125
Christian People's Movement (Madagascar), 117, 125
Churchill, (Sir) Winston S., 17, 135
Cities, see Urban development
Citröen, André, 93

Clemenceau, Georges, 118, 156
Cochinchina, 25–7, 52, 63, 69–70, 82, 89, 99–100
Colonial Congress (1904), 44
Colonial Congress (1906), 48
Colonial Empire, French, see Association Policy; Development of Colonies; Empire; France Overseas (under France); Military influences; Native aspirations; Urban development; Decolonization
Colonial Exhibition (Marseilles – 1906), 18
Comité de Vigilance des Intellectuelles Antifascists (1936), 118
Communication systems, see Air; Railway; Sea routes
Communism, 118, 119, 120, 141–2
    see also Ho Chi Minh
Compagnie des Messageries Maritime, 92
Compagnie Maritime des Chargeurs Réunis, 92
Companies set up overseas, 77–8
Conakry, 112
Confédération des Travailleurs (Tunisia), 126
Congo, 34, 85
Congress Against Imperialism and Colonial Oppression (Brussels – 1927), 118
Constantine, City of, 98, 143
Corvée principle, 82
Crozier, Michel, 73
Cullen, Countee, 123
Curzon of Kedleston, Marquess, 17

Dahomey, riots in, 126
Dakar, 77, 79, 87, 94–5, 100–3, 108–13, 125
    wartime bombardment of, 134
Darcy, Jean, 30
Daumier, Honoré, 41
Decolonization, 133–49:
    banishments, 142
    booknotes, 167–8
    Brazzaville Conference (1944), 136–7
    Central States in Africa, WW II importance of, 134
    collapse of 3rd Republic, 135
    community basis policy, 140–1, 148
    Defferre Law (1956), 139
    destruction of French Navy, 135
    Eurafrica proposals, 148–9
    FIDES scheme, 139–40
    Fifth Republic, 147, 148
    FLN Movement, 146
    Fourth Republic, 138, 140, 146–7
    French Union concept, 138–9
    independence, first claims for, 139
    loss of Algeria, 145–7
    loss of Vietnam, 145
    North African Campaign, 134–5, 142
    Post War II reconstruction, 137–49
    Vichy Régime, 134–6
    Viet Minh, 141–2, 145
Defferre Law, 139

De Gaulle, Charles, 13–14, 38, 52, 134–43, 147–8
Delafosse, Maurice, 74
Delavignette, Robert, 75, 81, 82, 84, 95, 112
Delcassé, Théophile, 25, 33
De Lesseps, Ferdinand, 31
Déroulède, Paul, 18
Deschamps, Hubert, 67, 80, 112, 155–6
Deschanel, Paul, 49
Development of Colonies, 74–96:
    agricultural basis, 76, 77
    airships, experiments with, 94
    air travel, 94–5
    booknotes, 162–4
    capital investment, attempts to make, 75–6, 78–9
    cars, advent of, 93–4
    companies and consortia, 77–8
    concession companies, 78, 80
    Corvée principle, 82
    Delavignette, 75, 81–2, 84, 95
    education, 84–8, 90
    effects of World War I, 74–5
    farmer settlers, 79
    federation policy, 92
    fortunes are hard to come by, 79–80
    home politics, effects of, 79
    illtreatment of natives, 81
    labour relations, 81–4, 90
    language, 88–90
    missionaries, 85
    natives as troops, 90–1
    racism, 82, 84
    railway construction, 83, 92
    recruiting and training of ex-patriates, 80–1
    road building programme, 94
    rubber trade, 77
    sea routes opened up, 92–3
    start of operations, 74
    trade, 76–7
Diagne, Blaise, 91, 103, 118, 127
Dien Bien Phu, 145
Dilke, Sir Charles, 53
Disease, 103, 104–5, 125
Disraeli, Benjamin, 41
DuBois, W. E. B., 117

Eboué, Félix, 88, 134
Ecole Cambodsienne, 88
Ecole Coloniale, 80, 88
Ecole William Ponty, Dakar, 87
Education, 84–8, 90
Egypt:
    campaign of 1798–9, 20
    colonial powers' rivalry over, 31–4
    trading activities (1870s), 27
El-Hadj Omar, 23, 60–1
Empire, growth of, from 1830–1919, 17–36:
    Algeria, first incursion into, 21, 23
    a start made in Africa, 22–4
    booknotes, 158–60
    Central Africa, 31–2

Cochinchina, 26–7
effect of Napoleon I's policy, 20
Egypt, trade relations with, 27–8, 31–2
Far East, activities in, 22, 25–7
German Agreement, 34
Indian enclaves, 27
Morocco, 24–5, 28, 33–4
railway systems, start of, 28–9
Samory, Empire of, 24
Senegal, start in, 23–4
situation in 1919, 35–6
start of 2nd colonial, 21–2
Tunisia, beginnings of, 28
War, 1914–18, effects of, 34–5
see also Decolonization; Development of
    Colonies; Imperialism; Native aspira-
    tions; Urban development; Military
    influences
Entente Cordiale (1903), 30, 33
Epidemics, 103, 104–5, 125
Etienne, Eugène, 34, 44, 75

Faidherbe, Louis, 23, 55, 60–2, 67, 150
Fall, Bernard, 144
Fanon, Frantz, 88, 153–4
Farmer settlers, 79, 112–13
Fashoda Incident, 32
Faure, Félix, 88
Federation policy, 92
Ferry, Jules, 19, 44, 47, 52, 69, 156
Feydeau, Ernest, 99
Fez, city of, 97
FIDES policy, 139–40
FLN Movement, 146
Force Noire, 90–1
Foreign Legion, 14
France:
    American possessions, 19–20
    Fifth Republic, 147, 148
    Fourth Republic, 138, 140, 146–7
    1939–45 War, 134–7
    'Overseas' (Outre-mer), 54, 90, 137, 149
        modern links with, 150–7:
            achievements in retrospect, 155
            compared with British Empire, 155–7
            economic aid, 151–2
            elite and masses contrasted, 154–5
            literature, 153–6
            subsidization policy, 151–2
            technical aid, 151
    Third Republic, collapse of, 135
    see also Association Policy; Decolonization;
        Development of Colonies; Imperialism;
        Military influences; Native aspirations;
        Urban development
Francophony, 150
Franco-Prussian War (1870), 18
Freycinet, Charles de, 32

Gabon, 22, 31, 32, 85, 134
Gallieni, General Joseph, 55–6, 60, 62–5, 67,
    72

Gambetta, Léon, 32
Garnier, François, 25–6
Garvey, Marcus T., 125
Gaud-Toqué Affair, 81
Germany, diplomatic crisis with, over
    Morocco, 65
    war with (1870), 18
Gide, André, 84, 118
Gilson, Etienne, 38
Girardet, Raoul, 156
Goncourt Prize, 116
Guadeloupe, 19, 79, 88, 102
Guèye, Lamine, 124–5
Guiana, French, 19
Guinea, 141, 148

Hadj, Messali, 118, 121, 128–31, 143
Hanoi, 25–6, 63, 88, 111, 126, 130, 144
Hanotaux, Gabriel, 29, 71–2
Hardy, Georges, 62
Harlem Renaissance, 122–3
Harmand, Jules, 50–1, 69
Hatta, Mohammed, 118
Herriot, Edouard, 139
Ho Chi Minh, 121–2, 127, 129–30, 141–2,
    144
    see also Indochina; Hanoi; Tonkin
Holy Ghost Fathers, 85
Hué, City of, 97
Hué, Treaty of (1883–4), 69–70
Hughes, Langston, 122–3
Humbert, Senator Charles, 39

Illtreatment, 81
Imperialism, early 20th cent. theories of, 37–
    53:
    absorption policy, 39–40, 48, 51
    association, new policy of, 49, 51
    booknotes, 160–1
    Britain, Germany and America contrasted,
        37–8, 40, 44
    'brutalists', 49–51
    conservative outlook, 43–4
    contemporary thinkers, 41
    economy, 45–6
    expansionist views, 47, 52
    Harmand's attitude, 50–1
    La Plus Grande France, 52–3
    Leroy-Beaulieu's essay, 40–1, 45–6
    life or death concept, 40–1
    Marxist tradition, 46–7
    Mill (J. S.), views of, adapted, 44–6
    Mission Civilisatrice, 39, 49
    'Native Policy', 48–50
    neurasthenia, 40
    'new imperialism', 45
    Sarraut's views, 40
    settlement policy abandoned, 47
    sociological aspects, 47–8
    Thomist view, 38
Indochina:
    annexation of (1859), 22

community policy opposed, 141–4
Corvée principle, 82
expansionist ideas, 47
French attempts to avoid direct rule, 68–9
Gallieni's military control, 55, 59, 63
Garnier's trade expedition, 25–6
nationalism, start of, 124–5
railway, 92
Rivière's work in, 26
rubber industry of, 77
settler farmers in, 79
today's links with France, 154
World War II and, 135
see also Annam; Cochinchina; Hanoi; Ho
    Chi Minh; Saigon; Vietnam
International Colonial Exposition (1931), 97,
    106, 122, 123, 157
International Congress of Colonial Sociology
    (1900), 48
International Debt Commission, 28
International Labor Organization, 83
Isly, Battle of (1844), 23
Ivory Coast, 27

Jaurès, Mons., 119
Jonnart, Charles, 106

Kaiouran, 97
Khaled, Emir, 124
Khedive, The (Ismael Pasha), 27, 31

Labour relations, 81–4, 90, 126–7
La Morcière, General, 110
Lamothe, Henri de, 111
Lanessan, Jean de, 70, 100
Languages, 88–90, 150
Latécoère, Pierre, 94–5
Lavigerie, Charles, 85
Laye, Camara, 85
League of Nations, 35, 83
Lebanon, 34, 35, 135
Le Bon, Gustave, 50
Leclerc, General, 134, 147
Le Corbusier, Mons., 109–10
Léro, Etienne, 123
Leroy-Beaulieu, Paul, 40–1, 45–6, 51, 71
Levant, 20
Leyguès, Georges, 48
Lipton, Thomas, 79
Literature, African, 116, 117, 122–3, 153–6
    see also individual names of writers as
        Césaire, Senghor, etc.
Louisiana sale (1803), 20
Louis-Philippe, King, 56–7
Lugard Memorial Lecture, 1963, 154–5
Lyautey, Hubert, 23, 25, 55–6, 60, 63, 64,
    70–3, 80, 100, 106–7, 157
Lyautey, Pierre, 36
Lyons, City of, commercial trade with Far
    East from, 27

MacKay, Claude, 123

Madagascar:
    Gallieni and Lyautey in, 55–6, 63–5, 72–3
    labour relations, 82–3
    nationalism in, 125–6
    rebellion (1947), 147
    settlers in, 79
    today's links with France, 154
    World War II, 135
Mager, Henri, 44
Mahdists, 32
Malagasy, see Madagascar
Malraux, André, 118
Mangin, Lt. Col. Georges, 91
Maran, René, 116
Marchand, Jean-Baptiste, 31–3
Maritime development, 92–3
Marquette, Père, 85
Marsa, Treaty of (1883), 71
Marseilles, Exhibition at, 18
Martinique, 19, 79, 136, 153–4
Martonne, Edouard de, 90–1
Marx, Karl, 46, 47, 79
Massis, Henri, 41
Massu, General, 147
Maximilian, Emperor of Mexico, 18, 20
Medusa (frigate), 22
Mehemet Ali, 31
Melia, Jean, 118
Memmi, Albert, 153–4
Merina peoples, see Madagascar
Merivale, Herman (1806–74), 46
Merlin, Jean, 125
Mers-el-Kabir, naval action at, 135
Messimy, Albert, 29, 91
Military influences over colonies, 54–73:
    association policy, 67, 68, 73
    booknotes, 161–2
    Bugeaud in Algeria, 55–60
    Cochinchina, 68–9, 70
    Faidherbe in Senegal, 60–2
    Gallieni's time, 62–5, 72
    Hanataux's view, 72
    Indochina, 63, 65, 68
    Lyautey's time, 64, 66–7, 71–3
    Madagascar, 55–6, 63–5, 72–3
    Military control, early days of, 55–60
    Morocco, 65–7, 71
    'Overseas France', 54
    resistance, pockets of, 54–5
    Treaty of Marsa (1883), 71
    Tunisia, 71
Millet, René, 33
Miquelon, 134
Missionaries, activities of, 22, 63, 85
Mobile, USA, 97
Mohammed Ali, 126
Monicef, Bey of Tunis, 142
Montreal, 97, 150
Moors of Senegal, 60
Morocco, 23, 24–5, 28:
    and Germany, 34
    diplomatic crisis in, 65, 91

independence of, 147–8
Istiqlal Party in, 142
Lyautey in, 64–7
military rule in, 56
1942 assault on, 135
rivalry with Britain over, 33
Moulay Youssef, Sultan of Morocco, 67
Moutet, Marius, 79, 119
Mus, Paul, 133

Napoleon Bonaparte, 20–1
Nardal, Andrée, 123
Nationalism, see Native aspirations
National School for Overseas France, 75
Native aspirations, rise of, 116–31:
   booknotes, 165–7
   communism, 118, 119, 120
      see also Ho Chi Minh
   imperialism questioned, 118–19
   inter-war period, 116–26
   literature, 116, 117, 122–3
   modernist thought, 127–32
   nationalism, rise of, 118–22, 129
   Négritude, 121, 123–4
   Pan-Africanism, 117–18, 123
   Popular Front at home, 119–20
   strike weapon, 126
   Vietnam, 1930 revolt in, 126
   Youth Movements, 117
   see also names of individuals, as Bourguiba,
      Habib, Césaire, Aimé
'Native Policy', 48–50, 55, 58, 62, 68
Négritude, 121, 123–4
   see also Senghor, Léopold
Neo-colonialism, 150–7
New Caledonia, 38, 74
New Orleans, USA, 97
Nineteenth Century (journal), 17
Nguyen Ai Quoc (Ho Chi Minh), 121–2,
   127, 129, 130
Nguyen An Ninh, 125, 130
Nouira, Hedi, 127

Oppenheimer, J. Harry, 79
Oran, 98, 110
Oujda, unrest in, 113
Outlook (American Magazine), 38

Pan-Africanism, 117–18, 123
Paris Exposition (1937), 131
Paris Peace Conference (1919), 117, 121
Péguy, Charles, 41
Pétain, Marshal Philippe, 135
Phan Boi Chau, 117, 130
Picot, Georges, 35
Pinet-Laprade, Jean-Marie, 102, 105
Poincaré, Raymond, 66
Point-à-Pitre, 102
Pondicherry, 27
Prost, Henri, 107, 111
Protectorate policy, see Military influences
Prudhomme, Jacques, 18–19

Psichari, Ernest, 41, 74, 95

Racism, 90
Railways, 28–9, 83, 92, 126
Randau, Robert, 102
Ras-el-Ain episode (1904), 25
Régismanset, Charles, 50
Rhodes, Albert de, 85
Rhodes, Cecil, 44, 79
Rivière, Henri, 25–6
Roume, Ernest, 92, 101

Saigon, 98–100, 111
   see also Ho Chi Minh; Indochina; Vietnam
Saint-Exupéry, Antoine de, 95
St Louis, Réunion, 102
St Louis, Senegal, 102
Saint-Pierre Island, 134
Salafiyya Movement, 129
Samory, Empire of, 24
Sarraut, Albert, 40, 68, 75, 83, 87, 89, 90,
   118, 127
Sartre, Jean-Paul, 154
Schools, 84–8, 90
   see also under Ecole
Schumpeter, Joseph, 22
Schweitzer, Albert, 152–3
Sea routes, development of, 92–3
Segou, 24
Seillière, Ernest, 51
Senegal, 22–4
   military control of, 55
   modern links with France, 154
   railways of, 29
   under Faidherbe, 60–2, 150
Senghor, Léopold Sédar, 88, 121, 123–4, 128,
   131, 139, 148, 150
Smith, Adam, 46–7
Société Commerciale de L'Ouest Africain, 77
Soustelle, Jacques, 149
Staley, Eugene, 151
Sudan, 31, 63
Suez Canal, 27, 31–2, 92
Sun Yat-sen, 125, 130
Sykes, Sir Mark, 35
Syria, 27, 34–5:
   railway, 29
   World War II, 135

Tahiti (1843), 22
Talleyrand, Charles Maurice de, 19–20
Tananarive, 111, 127–8
Tarde, André, 41
Thiers, Adolphe, 56
Tillion, Germaine, 149, 151
Timbuctu, 97, 107
Togo(land), 35, 148
Tokolor peoples, 23–4
Tonkin, 25–6, 52, 63, 69–70, 80, 126, 130
Torrens, 44–5
Toussaint, Mons., 108, 110
Towns, see Urban development

Trade, attempts to develop, 76–7
Treaties:
    Hué, 69–70
    Marsa, 71
    with Merina Monarchy, 72
Tsiranana, Philibert, 140
Tunis, 17
Tunisia:
    expansion ideas in, 47
    French occupation of (1881), 28, 52
    nationalism, rise of, 125
    post World War II, 142, 147–8
    railways of, 29
    Treaty of Marsa (1883), 71
    see also Bourguiba, Habib
'Two Town' concept, 107, 110–11

Upper Niger, 63
Urban development, 97–115:
    architecture, 101–2, 104, 106
    booknotes, 164–5
    buildings, new styles of, 101–2
    cities, beginnings of, 98
    concrete, introduced, 108
    depression of 1930s, effects of, 105, 113
    disease, 103, 104–5
    electricity introduced, 105
    European Settlement, lack of, 112–13
    lack of central control from Paris, 111
    military, barracks for, 104
    monuments, 106, 150
    native servants, 105
    post World War II, 111–15
    provincialism, 112
    road-paving, 103

sewerage, 103
shops, theatres and cinemas, 104–5
slow rate of progress, 102
social pattern, 103–5
town planning, 102, 105–6, 108
traffic control, 108
trams and buses, 105
'two town' concept, 107, 110–11
water, problems of, 103
see also names of individual towns and
    cities, as Saigon

Van Vollenhoven Joost, 74
Varennes, Alexandre, 124
Verne, Jules, 28, 29
Vichy Regime, 134–6
Viet Minh, 141–2, 145, 151
Vietnam Republic, 142, 143–4
    see also Indochina; Hanoi; Tonkin
Viollette, Maurice, 119, 130
Vy Vato Sakelike Movement, 125, 126

Wakefield, Edward Gibbon, 44–5
War, 1914–18, 34–5, 74–5, 90–1, 117, 120
War, 1939–45, 95–6, 133
    development activities after, 111–15
    see also Decolonization
Ward, Barbara, 151
Washington, Booker T., 125
Weithas, Colonel E., 111
White Fathers Order, 85

Young Algerian/Tunisian Movements, 117,
    125, 129
Youth Party in Vietnam, 117